FOLK
MITTENS

TECHNIQUES AND PATTERNS FOR
HANDKNITTED MITTENS

MARCIA LEWANDOWSKI

INTERWEAVE PRESS

Cover design, Susan Wasinger, Signorella Graphic Arts
Photography, Joe Coca
Technical editing, Dorothy T. Ratigan

Interweave Press
201 East Fourth Street
Loveland, Colorado 80537
USA

Printed in Hong Kong by Sing Cheong

Library of Congress Cataloging-in-Publication Data

Lewandowski, Marcia, 1958–
    Folk Mittens: techniques and patterns for handknitted mittens /
by Marcia Lewandowski
        p.   cm.
    Includes bibliographical references and index.
    ISBN 1-883010-34-9
    1. Knitting—Patterns.   2. Mittens.   I. Title.
TT825.L4447   1997
746.42'20432—dc21   97-9475
                                                      CIP

First printing: IWP—10M:697:CC

For my family,

Rory, Abbey, and Nate,

who through many winters have learned to

depend on and appreciate the warmth and

beauty of the humble folk mitten.

Contents

Introduction

"There were hills which garnished their heights with stately trees; humble valleys whose base estate seemed comforted with refreshing silver rivers; meadows enameled with all sorts of eye-pleasing flowers: thickets which, being lined with the most pleasant shade, were witnessed so to be by the cheerful preposition of many well-tuned birds; each pasture stored with sheep feeding in sober security, while the pretty lambs, with oratory, craved the dams' comfort, here a shepherd's boy piping as though he should never be old; there a young shepherdess knitting and withal singing, and it seemed that her voice comforted her hands to work and her hands kept time to her voice's music."

—Sir Philip Sidney, *Arcadia*, 1577

Knitting has always been, to its very roots, a practical art, with craftsmanship grounded in inventiveness, utility, and common sense. For centuries, harsh climates around the world inspired the knitting of wool garments that provided an unrivaled defense from the elements. Yet handknitted garments were created for more than winter protection. They were knit to express care for the wearer, to identify homeland and family, to fulfill traditions of courtship and marriage, to follow fashion, to increase family income, or simply for the sheer pleasure of giving expression to creative talents. All this and more can be seen in the humble mitten.

I began this book project by collecting historical mitten patterns. The collection soon expanded to include other beautiful ethnic patterns that I found knit into gloves, socks, shawls, caps, and sweaters. I looked for patterns that had small design elements with frequent repeats that could be applied to mittens. In northern Europe, many motifs were well documented and I had great freedom in choosing among them. In other areas, such as eastern Europe and the Near East, records were less thorough and my pattern choices were limited. I was disappointed in my search for the rumored rich knitting traditions of the Himalayas, and found only one pattern which originated with the Kashmiri people of India.

For the purpose of this book, I use the terms "folk knitters" and "peasant knitters" to include those knitters of old who often found their greatest outlet to creative expression in designing knitted garments. Many knitting cultures derived a sense of identity from their designs and chose to guard their unique techniques and patterns. Others freely shared with neighboring cultures, and the patterns would change, taking on distinctly regional characteristics.

It was interesting to find identical designs in widely separated locations, each considered traditional to that area. For example, the familiar Nordic eight-point rose or star was also knit in the Middle East, known there as the Eastern Star, symbolizing the four sacred elements of earth, air, sun, and water. Textiles in Rome also incorporated the star as a symbol of rebirth.

Knitting folk mittens is not difficult. With knowledge of the basics, all you need are needles and a few ounces of yarn. Knitting ethnic mittens connects us with other people and cultures. The stories and bits of folklore that accompany the endlessly varying patterns comprise national legacies. This book contains just a sampling of the world's wealth of patterns. We may be inspired by and become part of these living traditions by adding our own valuable insights and experience, from which future knitters will benefit.

Early History of Knitting

The craft of knitting as we know it today, using two or more needles, evolved over many centuries. Its earliest roots have been found among the Arabian nomads. From there it moved east to India, where evidence shows knitting flourished before the eleventh century. It then moved along North Africa into Spain. From Spain, knitting spread throughout Europe. Accurate dating of knitting and its place in history are difficult since knitted garments were made for practical use. When the clothing was no longer serviceable, the yarn was either reused or, if past salvaging, discarded, and the organic fibers of wool, cotton, silk, and linen readily decomposed.

Equipment and Techniques

Yarn

One of the most enjoyable parts of knitting is the selection of yarn from the many colors and textures available. But remember, not all yarn is created equal. Your mittens will be no better than the yarn you use.

The labor of making a folk mitten deserves materials of the highest quality. Synthetic, oil-based fibers were created as a substitute for pure natural fibers. But I view them as just that—substitutes. Wool is a naturally renewable fiber as old as history itself and traditionally used by folk knitters. Wool is gathered from a wide variety of animals, most notably sheep. In some cultures, sheep were considered more useful than the family cow—they supplied wool as well as milk and meat. Of secondary importance were fibers from goat, llama, alpaca, camel, yak, and rabbit, to name a few.

Wool has a natural ability to resist absorption of moisture, insulate against heat and cold, resist flame, and maintain its resilience. Even so, wool can absorb as much as 30 percent of its weight in moisture without feeling wet to the touch, compared with cotton at 8 percent and synthetics at less than 5 percent. An added bonus is that as wool goes from dry to wet, it gives off warmth, with a single gram of wool producing twenty-seven calories of heat.

Lanolin, an oil secreted by sheep that is a popular ingredient in hand lotions, lends wool its excellent water-repellency. It also softens the hands of both the knitter and the mitten wearer. Wool, more than any other fiber, is a bit forgiving of the knitter—if the mitten does not fit the intended wearer perfectly, washing and blocking can change its size and shape. The shrinking or felting that occurs when a woolen garment is incorrectly exposed to heat, cold, moisture, and agitation is viewed as a drawback, yet for centuries, folk cultures have used this property of wool to their advantage. Felted wool creates an even warmer, more water-repellent garment.

Washing Wool

Properly washing wool to avoid felting is not difficult. Wash a wool mitten by hand in lukewarm water with a mild soap, and use water of the same temperature to rinse. Do not twist or rub, instead squeeze or knead the wool while washing. After rinsing, press out excess moisture, roll the mitten up in a towel, and leave it there for fifteen minutes. On a dry towel, shape the mitten to size and allow it to dry away from direct heat and out of the sun.

Felting Wool

Felting mats the fibers of the wool and results in a warmer, more solid mitten. Any wool mitten can be felted. Allow for 5 to 10 percent shrinkage and be aware that mittens will shrink more in length than in width. To felt, lather the mittens using soap and hot water. (Some cultures used hot fish broth.) Scrub each mitten for about five minutes. Then rinse in icy cold water. Check the size and continue the washing and rinsing process until the desired fit is achieved. One tablespoon of ammonia in the rinse water helps soften the wool. Block and dry as usual.

Colors

Some folk knitters favored bold, vivid colors to brighten their stark winter environments. Others chose earthy hues, enjoying their warmth and gentleness. As far as possible, each mitten in this book was knit in colors typical of the culture it came from.

Needles

Folk knitters used double-pointed needles, which allowed them to work garments in the round, smoothly connecting one round with the next. Knitters of old would have little patience for the modern method of sewing up seams. Some patterns today even call for the fingers of gloves to be knit in rectangles and later sewn up!

When knitting in the round, the right side of the fabric always faces the knitter so the pattern can be seen at all times. This is especially valuable for the more complex folk patterns. Working stockinette stitch in the round, you knit every round, rather than alternating knit and purl rows as when knitting on straight needles. The knitting goes faster and the tension is more uniform when every stitch is knit. The absence of seams makes a garment stronger and eliminates the tedium of sewing sections together. Small garments such as mittens are knit with four or five double-pointed needles. Sweaters may be knit with eight to ten needles, which allows two people to work on the same garment simultaneously. All the mittens in this book are designed to be knit in the round on double-pointed needles.

Using Double-Pointed Needles

Cast all stitches onto one needle. If using four needles, divide stitches evenly over three needles, and use the fourth to begin the knitting. If using five needles (preferred by most folk knitters), spread stitches over four needles and use the fifth for knitting. Arrange needles to form a triangle or square, being careful that the cast-on edge is not twisted.

Pick up needles so that the needle with the first cast-on stitch is held in the left hand. Insert the free

Divide stitches evenly over three or four needles.

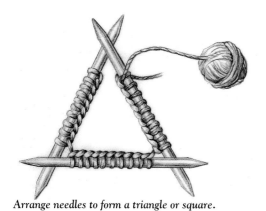

Arrange needles to form a triangle or square.

Gauge

needle into the first stitch on the left-hand needle and knit. This joins the circle and the first row of the pattern begins. When you reach the end of the first needle, the newly liberated needle is used to begin knitting the stitches on the next needle. At the end of the third needle (or fourth if knitting with five needles), the first row is completed. When beginning the first stitch of any needle, be mindful of the tension. Knitting the beginning stitch with slightly more tension helps eliminate the ladder effect that may occur at these transition points.

Gauge is the number of stitches in each inch (2.5 cm) of a knitted row. At the beginning of each of the patterns, a gauge is given. The importance of knitting with a correct gauge cannot be stressed enough if good-looking, well-fitting mittens are to result.

To check your gauge, cast on thirty stitches with the yarn selected for the mittens on the suggested needle size. Knit a length about three inches (7.5 cm) in stockinette stitch or the combination of stitches called for in the mitten pattern. While knitting the swatch, do not try to achieve the gauge, just knit comfortably. Smooth out the swatch and measure two inches (5 cm) in the center portion, including any half stitches. If the count has more stitches than needed, switch to larger needles; if the count has less than called for, try smaller needles. Do not assume that your next set of needles will achieve the correct gauge; keep making swatches until you get the correct gauge.

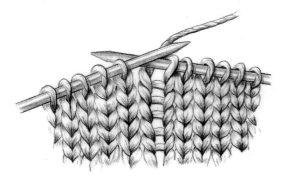

If the first stitch of a needle is knit with insufficient tension, the ladder effect may result.

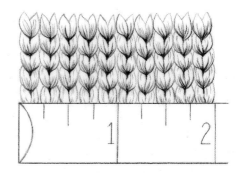

Smooth out the swatch and measure two inches (5 cm) in the center portion.

Long-Tail Cast-On

Make a slip knot and place on a needle, leaving a long tail. Place your thumb and index finger between the two threads and hold the long ends with your other fingers. Hold your hand with your palm facing upwards, and spread your thumb and index finger apart so that the yarn forms a V.

Insert the needle into the yarn around your thumb, from front to back.

Place the needle over the yarn around your index finger and bring the needle down through the loop around your thumb.

Drop the loop off your thumb and, placing your thumb back in the V configuration, tighten up the stitch on the needle.

Knotted Cast-On

Two-Color Cast-On

Leaving tails about 4" (10 cm) long, tie the two yarns together in an overhand knot. With your right hand, hold the knot on top of the needle a short distance from the tip, then place one yarn over your index finger and the other over your thumb. Continue as for a long-tail cast-on (bring the needle up through the loop on your thumb, hook it around the yarn on your finger, and back through the loop on your thumb). The yarn held on your index finger will make the stitches on the needle, the yarn held on your thumb will make the horizontal ridge at the base of the cast-on row.

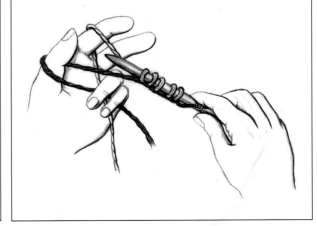

Casting On

There are many ways to cast on. Choose a cast-on stitch that is elastic and flexible. A good choice is the long-tail cast-on that uses a tail of one-half inch (1.25 cm) per cast-on stitch. For example, for a mitten with sixty stitches, a tail of thirty inches (76 cm) is sufficient.

The knitted jerseys of the European fisher folk used a variation of the long-tail cast-on called a knotted cast-on. First, make two long-tail cast-on stitches. The first stitch is then lifted over the second stitch and off the needle. The remaining stitch is the first knotted cast-on stitch. Cast on two more stitches and repeat to make the second cast-on stitch. Allow twice as long a yarn tail as in making the long-tail cast-on. This variation is hard-wearing and slightly decorative.

Plaited Edging

Plaiting is a northern European tradition that uses two colors to make a decorative twisted edge for two or more rounds. This technique discourages cuff edges from curling. Plaiting is worked in two colors with the purl side facing outward. Cast on the allotted number of stitches using both colors, one color over your index finger, the other over your thumb. The color that is over your index finger is the color that will be on the needle, the color over your

Plaiting creates a decorative edge.

thumb is the color that will form the horizontal ridge at the base of the cast-on edge. Plaiting is done by alternating two colors of yarn stitch for stitch while purling. The first stitch is purled with one color and then the yarn is dropped in front of the work. The second stitch is purled with the second color and that yarn is dropped in front of the work. The third stitch is purled with the first color, the fourth with the second, and so on. On some rounds the yarn to be used for the next stitch is lifted over the previous yarn, on other rounds, it is lifted under the previous one. In general, each stitch is worked with the same color yarn that was used in the previous round, but in some cases the alternate color is used. The specific techniques used for the plaited edgings on the mittens in this book are described with the mitten patterns.

Cuffs

Mitten cuffs are either ribbed or unribbed.

Ribbed Cuff

The ribbed cuff is the first choice of most mitten makers. It is snug and elastic, it doesn't curl, and it is easy to do. It is worked in a combination of knit and purl stitches. Popular ribbings include 2x2 (knit 2, purl 2), 3x1 (knit 3, purl 1), and 1x1 (knit 1, purl 1) ribs, all of which make superior cuffs. Many knitters use smaller needles for the ribbing than for the main body to produce a snugger fit. The ribbing may be lengthened or shortened to suit the knitter or wearer.

Bicolored corrugated ribbing makes a very decorative cuff. It is usually done in 2x2 rib. The knit stitches are worked in one color and the purl in a contrasting color. The yarn carried behind when not in use tends to decrease the ribbing's elasticity, making a firmer fabric.

Unribbed Cuff

The plain or "peasant" cuff is popular in traditional knitting. It is knit in stockinette stitch and allows for patterning that adds ethnic charm. The major drawbacks of this cuff are a looser fit and a bottom edge that tends to curl. The most common technique to minimize edge curling is to rib the first two to four rows before beginning the cuff patterning. Plaiting, hemming, or a lining may also be used to prevent curling.

Unribbed Cuff with Hem or Lining

Great Britain is one of the regions where a knitted hem or cuff lining was traditionally used. A hem or cuff lining is knit before the cuff is knit. About 90 percent of the cuff's stitch count is cast on and knit the length the cuff will be. A hem can vary between a few rounds to a more generous two-inch (5-cm) length. The last round is purled, creating an edge for neat turning. A picot turning edge is another option. Simply substitute the purl round with a sequence of knit two together, yarn over. This edge requires an even number of stitches.

Hems may be knit plain, or a name, date, design, or secret message may be worked into the knitting or added later with Swiss darning. After the mitten is complete, the hem is turned up and slip-stitched into place. This produces a warmer cuff of double thickness with an edge that won't curl, but it is not as elastic as a ribbed cuff.

Note: Most of the patterns included in this book call for an increase in stitches between the cuff and the mitten body. These increases are shown charted together on the left side of the mitten body chart, but they are to be spread evenly along the first row of the mitten body.

Thumbs

The thumb is the most challenging part of mitten making. For a good fit, you must knit to the shape of the human hand, which gradually widens to the thumb and abruptly narrows where the thumb branches off. The patterning and decreasing of the mitten body must be considered. These factors will affect whether the mittens need to have both right- and left-hand thumbs, or if a single thumb position will serve for both hands. Two basic ways of dealing with thumbs have evolved—the peasant or set-in thumb and the gore or gusset thumb.

Tradition and patterning dictate which thumb I use in each mitten. As you become comfortable with the charts, you will see how easily thumb styles can be changed and modified to suit your preference.

Peasant Thumb

This type of thumb has no gore and is the simplest to knit. Knit the mitten body up to the point where the thumb begins. Then use a length of contrasting waste yarn to knit the stitches where the thumb is to be placed. Place these stitches back onto the left needle and resume the body pattern with the main yarn, knitting the waste yarn stitches first. The waste yarn holds the stitches for the thumb and will later be removed. Once the body is finished, remove the waste yarn to begin the thumb. The loose stitches from the round above and the round below are slipped onto two needles and then rearranged onto

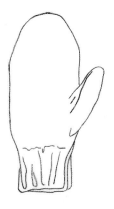

Peasant thumb	*Side seam gore*	*Normal gore*	*Norwegian gore*

three (or four if working with five needles). Some knitters prefer to slide the thumb stitches onto needles before removing the yarn length, allowing for a more orderly pick-up of stitches.

Most patterns call for additional stitches to be picked up on either side of the held stitches. Picking up extra stitches at the stress points where the thumb joins the body of the mitten is a trick many knitters use to avoid gaps and widen the thumb at the joint. These extra stitches are knit together on the following round to return to the correct number of stitches.

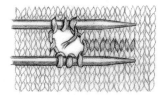

Once the body is finished, the waste yarn is removed, exposing thumb stitches which are slipped onto two needles and then rearranged onto three or four.

If a thumb pattern is a continuation of the body pattern, begin by knitting across the front-facing portion of the thumb to restore the correct pattern sequence then continue across the mitten hand. Because the peasant thumb has no gore, it interrupts the patterning only slightly; but without a thumb gore, the mitten makes no allowance for the varying width of the hand. It is knit straight up and tends to be boxy and inflexible.

Thumb Gores

Thumb gores accommodate the increase in hand width and therefore provide a better fit. There are three main types of gores, all of which begin at the wrist with one of the body stitches. Make-one (M1) increases (see illustration on page 17) are made at regular intervals, usually every two or three rounds, on either side of the forming thumb gore. When the thumb gore is long and wide enough (as specified in the chart), these stitches are placed on a length of yarn and held to be worked as the thumb later. The work on the mitten body is resumed by casting on a stitch over the gap made by the held stitches (to replace the initial stitch used in the gore), and then rejoining the work. When the body is complete, the waste yarn is removed and the exposed stitches are distributed over three or four needles. Additional stitches are usually picked up at the cast-on stitch and at each side to avoid gaps, achieve correct sizing, and bring the thumb stitch count to the number needed for patterning.

Side Seam Gore

This gore is placed at the inner edge or side seam of the mitten. Because the thumb will stick out of the side of the mitten, there is no difference between the left and the right mitten, except sometimes in the patterning. The advantage to this type of gore is that the body design is not interrupted. The disadvantage is a less-than-perfect fit because our thumbs do not grow out of the sides of our hands.

Normal Gore

This type of gore is located slightly into the palm of the hand, more in keeping with the location of the thumb. This allows for the best fitting mittens but interrupts the body patterning. Depending on the patterning and finishing, mittens may be ambidextrous or made for right and left hands. For example, if the top is decreased with the round decrease, the mitten can be ambidextrous.

Norwegian Gore

This variation uses aspects of both the peasant thumb and the normal thumb gore. Gore increases are made only on the palm side. When the gore is the required length, the gore stitches are knit onto a length of contrasting waste yarn (to be picked up later for the thumb), slipped back to left needle, and the mitten body is continued. The thumb is knit by

removing the yarn length and picking up the loose stitches from both the upper and lower rows, as for the peasant thumb. Additional stitches are picked up on the sides to prevent holes and widen the thumb for patterning as needed. This type of thumb is well positioned and there is no boxiness to the mitten shape. Traditionally, the gore has its own unique patterning. A right and a left mitten must be knit.

Note: Many knitters prevent gaps and widen the thumb as needed by picking up extra stitches at the stress points where the thumb joins the body of the mitten. These additional stitches are knit together on the following round to return to the correct number of stitches for patterning. This trick is not mentioned in any of the mitten instructions; it is up to you to decide whether or not to do it.

Top Decreases

There are two ways to shape the top of a mitten or thumb: with a round decrease or a flat decrease. In choosing which method to use, I considered both tradition and how the decreases would affect the patterning of the mitten body and thumb. Usually, decreases in the body begin when the mitten reaches the tip of the little finger. Thumb decreases begin when the piece measures to the middle of the thumbnail.

Round Decrease

Shape a rounded top for the mitten body or thumb with equally distributed decreases. Divide stitches as evenly as possible over three needles or, less often, four. At the end of each needle, two stitches are knit together, usually every two or three rounds. Keep in mind that these decreases may disrupt the patterning. At the top of the mitten or thumb, break the yarn leaving a six-inch (15-cm) tail. Thread the tail through the remaining stitches and draw it up to close the hole. A mitten with a rounded top can be shaped to fit either the right or left hand, or it can remain unshaped and suitable to both.

Round decrease

Flat Decrease

A flat decrease makes an angular top that can be squared off or end in a point. Ideally, use five needles with the palm section stitches evenly distributed on two and the back stitches on the other two. If only four needles are available, the third needle is used to hold all the back stitches. Make four de-

creases each round by decreasing two stitches on each side of the mitten. When the chart indicates a right-slanting decrease, simply knit two stitches together. If a left-slanting decrease is designated, use the ssk decrease (slip one stitch as to knit, slip the next stitch as to knit, then knit the two slipped stitches together through the back). For a pointed mitten top, continue decreasing until just a few stitches remain and draw them up together. For a mitten with a flat top, stop decreasing before a point is formed and graft the remaining stitches together with the Kitchener stitch. Mittens with flat decreases

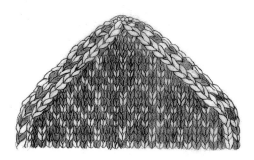

Flat decrease

Kitchener Stitch

Bring a threaded yarn needle through the front stitch as if to purl, leaving the stitch on the needle, then through the back stitch as if to knit, again leaving the stitch on the needle.

*Go back through the same front stitch as if to knit, and then slip this stitch off the needle. Bring the yarn needle through the next front stitch as if to purl, leaving the stitch on the needle, then through the first back stitch as if to purl, and slip that stitch off the needle. Pass the yarn needle through the next back stitch as if to knit, leaving the stitch on the needle. Repeat from * until no stitches remain.

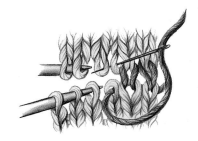

---

must almost always be knit left- or right-handed, because of the thumb placement. This angular style of decrease disrupts the mitten patterning only along the sides, where it is least noticeable. A small design may be knit between the decreases at the sides.

Eastern Knitting

All the knitters that I have met use the Western technique of knitting. The Eastern method is a refreshing variation and a challenge. Eastern knitting is commonly used throughout the Balkan countries into the Near East, predominantly in stocking production, but in mittens and gloves as well. I give instructions for one simple type of casting on. If you enjoy this method of knitting from the top down, there are other books available that explore the method in more detail. As you become comfortable using the Eastern method of knitting, you will find that any mitten pattern can be knit using this technique.

Use five double-pointed needles for this technique. To cast on, hold two double-pointed needles together, bring the tail to the front between the two needles and snugly wind the working yarn counterclockwise around the needles. Each wrap of the needles represents two potential stitches, so use half as many wraps as the number of stitches you want. After winding, bring the yarn forward between needles back to front. The first row begins by knitting across the upper needle. Bring the lower needle slightly to the right to ensure that you don't drop any stitches from it while completing stitches on the upper needle. Once you have knit across all stitches on the upper needle, rotate the work and knit across the same number of stitches on the other needle. On the third row, you will increase stitches and begin working with five

Eastern Knitting Setup

Snugly wrap the working yarn counterclockwise around two needles. Bring the yarn forward between needles, back to front.

Knit across stitches on upper needle.

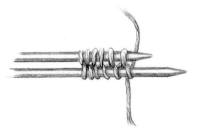

Rotate the work and knit across the same number of stitches on the other needle.

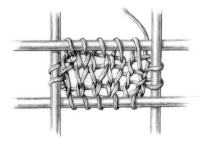

On the third row, pick up two stitches along each side.

M1 Increase

With left needle tip, lift the strand between the last knitted stitch and first stitch on the left needle.

Knit the lifted loop through the back of the loop.

needles. Work across the stitches on the first needle, then use a new needle to pick up two stitches from the gap between the two needles holding stitches. One of these new stitches is a palm stitch, the other a back stitch. Turn the work and use a new needle to knit the remaining stitches, then, using yet another needle, pick up two stitches from the gap as you did on the other side. Stitches are now held on four needles and the fifth needle is the working needle. Reposition the needles so that the stitches for the back of the mitten are evenly spread over two needles and the mitten palm stitches are evenly spread over the other two needles. Continue increasing, with M1 increases, one stitch each side of the back and one stitch each side of the palm stitches (four stitches total each round) as charted. Use these flat increases on both the body top and thumb tip.

Connecting Thumb to Mitten Body

The thumbs used in Eastern knitting are similar to the simple peasant thumb, but they are knit separately from the top down. Completely knit the thumb, place the stitches on two holders (half of the stitches on each), and then knit the body of the mitten to the point where the chart indicates the thumb should be joined. Place the inward-facing side of the thumb in position on the mitten body, lining up pairs of stitches. With the wrong side of the fabric facing you, join matching stitches by knitting together one stitch from the thumb holder with the corresponding stitch from the body. After two stitches have been worked, begin casting off. After the join is complete, place the outward-facing thumb stitches from the second holder onto the needles holding the mitten body, and continue the piece as charted to the cuff.

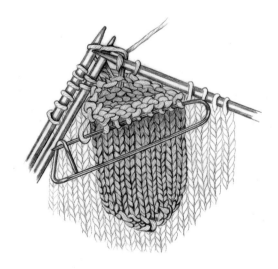

The thumb is joined to the mitten body by knitting together one stitch from the thumb holder with the corresponding stitch from the body.

Finger-Knit Mitten Cord

Mitten cords that are "finger knit" are sturdy and long-wearing. Once you have mastered the technique, you can do it with your eyes closed. Cords may be used to attach pairs of mittens to prevent the loss of one. Shorter cord lengths may also be used to make loops for buttons or for hanging.

To finger knit a cord, measure a length of yarn about nine times as long as the desired finished cord length. Make a slip knot in the center of the yarn length. (To make a cord that's attached to a mitten, thread the yarn through the edge of the mitten at the desired location and pull it half way through so that the two ends of the yarn are even. Make a slip knot on one of the yarns, as close to the mitten edge as possible.) Place your left index finger through the slip knot. In your right hand, hold the tail of yarn that tightens the knot when pulled; in your left hand, hold the tail of yarn that makes the loop. Insert your right index finger into the front of the loop, hook it under the yarn held in your right hand to form a new loop, and draw the loop through. Remove your left finger and hold the knot lightly in your right hand while you pull gently on the tail held in your left hand to tighten the first loop. Now, insert your left index finger into the front of the new loop, hook it under the yarn held in your left hand to form a new loop, and draw the new loop through. Remove your right finger, hold the knot gently in your left hand, and pull on the tail in your right hand to tighten the loop. Continue in this way, making loops of yarn from alternating yarn ends until the cord is the desired length. For a two-colored cord, tie two colors of yarn together with an overhand knot, then work as described above, holding

Two-Colored Finger-Knit Cord

Tie the two colors together with an overhand knot. Make a loop with the light yarn around a loop of the dark yarn. Place your left finger through the dark loop and hold the knot with your left thumb and middle finger. Pull the light yarn with your right hand to tighten the light loop close to the knot.

Insert your right index finger into the front of the loop held by your left finger, hook it under the light yarn held in your right hand, and draw the loop through. Remove your left finger and pull on the dark yarn to tighten the dark loop close to the knot.

Insert your left index finger into the front of the light loop held by your right finger, hook it under the dark yarn held in your left hand, and draw the loop through. Remove your right finger and pull on the light yarn to tighten the light loop close to the knot.

the dark yarn in one hand and the light yarn in the other.

Swiss Darning

Swiss darning, or duplicate stitching, is used to correct a misplaced stitch or to apply motifs that would otherwise involve long, awkward yarn carries. Duplicate stitches lie on top of the original stitches and appear to be knitted in.

Thread yarn on a blunt needle. Draw yarn from wrong to right side of the work at the center of the stitch below the stitch to be covered, leaving a three-inch (7-cm) tail to be woven in later. Following the outline of the stitch, insert the needle from right to left behind both sides of the stitch above the one

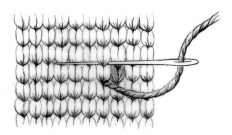

Draw yarn from wrong to right side at center of stitch below the one to be covered. Then insert needle from right to left behind both sides of the stitch above the one to be covered.

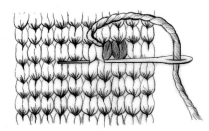

Insert the needle into center of same stitch below, then out through center of stitch to the left.

being duplicated. To complete the stitch, insert the needle into the center of the same stitch below, then out through the center of the stitch to the left. Allow the yarn to lie naturally; do not pull it tight.

Charts

Most folk patterns have been passed down through families and communities by word of mouth. In some cultures, girls were required to knit samplers that they could refer to later. If patterns were written, they were in chart form. Knitters of old were craftspeople who fashioned and improvised as they knit. Tiresome written directions are a modern invention and tend to be cumbersome. All mittens included in this book can be worked from the accompanying charts. Written instructions are brief and provided only for clarification. The basic instructions on increasing, decreasing, cuffs, and thumbs that are included in this section should be applied as needed.

The charts demonstrate the symmetry of most patterns. After your fingers learn the rhythm of a pattern, you will only need the chart occasionally.

Charts are read from right to left, beginning at the lower right corner and progressing upward. The charts for Eastern knitting appear upside down because the knitting progresses from the fingertips to the cuffs.

Mitten charts may show the entire mitten or just half. If only half the mitten is charted, both sides are identical (except for the placement of the thumb), including charted increases and decreases; two complete repeats of the chart should be worked. The increases shown between the cuff or ribbing and the mitten body should also be repeated. Increases made between the cuff and the body appear together in a block on the charts, but must be evenly spaced along the row.

The length of a ribbed cuff is up to you; the charts indicate only a ribbing style.

Finishing

Having lovingly knit a pair of mittens, don't compromise their charm by leaving loose yarn ends or holes at the thumb joints. Use a blunt needle to weave in all loose ends on the inside of the mitten. With matching yarn, reinforce any stress points, particularly the joints where the thumb is attached to the body. Finally, block the mittens by applying heat to smooth and even out the stitches. Folk knitters commonly blocked their mittens by placing them on their kitchen chairs for a few days and sitting on them while they ate their meals. A modern alternative is to turn the mitten inside out and lightly steam it through a damp cloth. Avoid blocking ribbings since steam tends to make ribbing lose its elasticity.

Sizing Mittens

The mittens in this book, with a few exceptions, are sized for a medium woman's hand. (See list of sizes below.) The patterns may easily be changed to fit any hand by changing the gauge. For fewer stitches per inch, use smaller needles or finer yarn; for more, use larger needles or bulkier yarn. The charts may also be altered by removing or adding a portion of the pattern vertically or horizontally.

The following measurements are for typical mitten sizes; however, the overall length of a mitten greatly depends on the length of its cuff. Every pair of hands is unique; adjust your mittens as needed.

Men's Large: 10 inches (25.5 cm) around; 10 inches (25.5 cm) long.

Men's Medium/Women's Large: 9 inches (23 cm) around; 9 to 10 inches (23 to 25.5 cm) long.

Men's Small/Women's Medium/Children's Large: 8 inches (20.5 cm) around; 8 to 9 inches (20.5 to 23 cm) long.

Women's Small/Children's Medium: 7 inches (18 cm) around; 7 to 8 inches (18 to 20.5 cm) long.

Children's Small: 6 inches (15 cm) around; 5 to 6 inches (12.5 to 15 cm) long.

Abbreviations	
beg	begin, beginning
BO	bind off
cn	cable needle
CO	cast on
cont	continue, continuing
dec, decs	decrease, decreasing, decreases
inc, incs	increase, increasing, increases
k	knit
m	marker
p	purl
pm	place marker
psso	pass slipped stitch over
rem	remaining
rnd, rnds	round, rounds
sl	slip
st, sts	stitch, stitches
St st	stockinette stitch
tbl	through back loop
tog	together

The Patterns

Basic Mittens

The Classic Mitten

If you are just beginning to try your hand at knitting mittens, consider starting with the simple classic mitten. This mitten is worked without pattern change, but includes thumb gore increases and top decreases so you can learn the basics and be ready to move on to more challenging patterns. The basic thumb gore is not complicated by a pattern stitch. Use any yarn that gives the correct gauge. Shown here is classic red yarn.

Finished Size: Children's small (children's medium, children's large, women's medium, men's medium).
Materials: 3 to 4 oz (85 to 113.5 g) worsted-weight wool; size 4 (3.5 mm) double-pointed needles.
Gauge: 10 sts = 2" (5 cm).

Mitten body: CO 32 (36, 40, 44, 48) sts. Join. Work 2x2 rib for desired length. Change to St st and

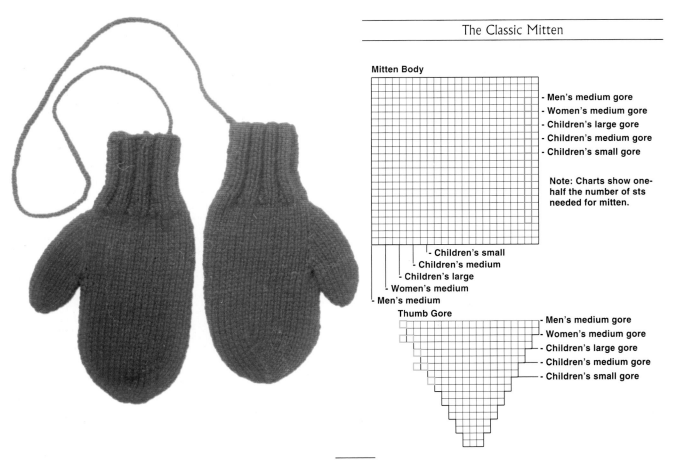

The Classic Mitten

Mitten Body

- Men's medium gore
- Women's medium gore
- Children's large gore
- Children's medium gore
- Children's small gore

Note: Charts show one-half the number of sts needed for mitten.

- Children's small
- Children's medium
- Children's large
- Women's medium
- Men's medium

Thumb Gore
- Men's medium gore
- Women's medium gore
- Children's large gore
- Children's medium gore
- Children's small gore

The Classic Mitten

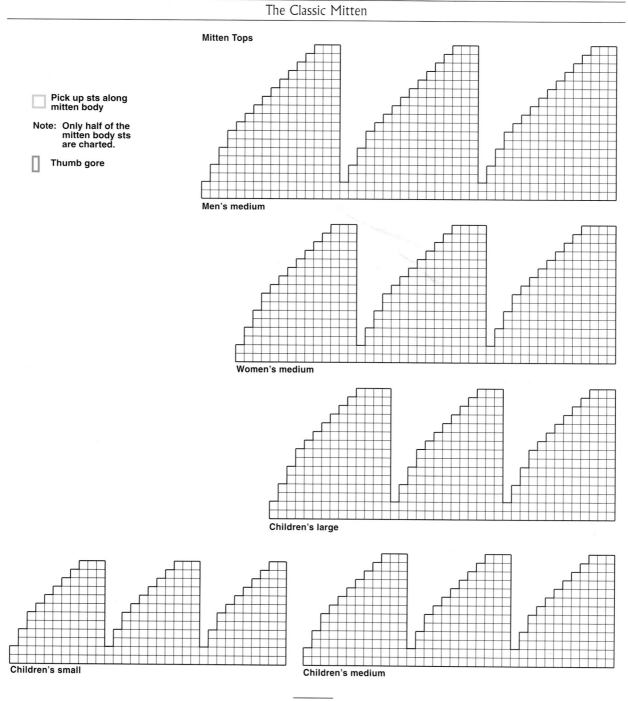

Mitten Tops

Pick up sts along mitten body

Note: Only half of the mitten body sts are charted.

Thumb gore

Men's medium

Women's medium

Children's large

Children's small

Children's medium

The Classic Mitten

Thumb Tops

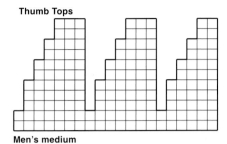

Men's medium

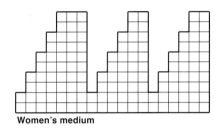

Women's medium

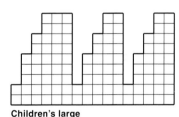

Children's large

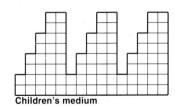

Children's medium

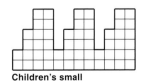

Children's small

work 3 rnds. On the next rnd, begin normal thumb gore and work as charted for 10 (12, 14, 16, 18) rnds—11 (13, 15, 17, 19) thumb sts. Place thumb sts on yarn length. Cont across rnd, CO 1 (1, 1, 1, 1) st over held thumb sts, and rejoin. Work even on 32 (36, 40, 44, 48) sts until piece measures to tip of little finger. Work 3-point dec as charted. Draw up rem sts. **Thumb:** Place thumb sts on needles, pick up 1 (2, 1, 2, 1) st(s) along the mitten body, and join— 12 (15, 16, 19, 20) sts. Work even until piece measures to middle of thumbnail. Work 3-point dec as charted. Draw up rem sts.

Lined Mittens

Lined mittens are basically two mittens that are joined together at the cuff—a lightweight inner mitten tucked inside a heavyweight outer mitten. They are snug and warm. Vertical repeating patterns are especially well suited for this type of mitten, although almost any pattern can be used. The inner mitten, only visible when pulled out for drying, can be plain or patterned, or even personalized with a message, name, or date.

Finished Size: 8 ½" (21.5 cm) around by about 9 ¾" (25 cm) long.

OUTER MITTEN
Materials: 2 oz (56.5 g) dark worsted-weight wool, 2 oz (56.5 g) light worsted-weight wool; size 5 (3.75 mm) double-pointed needles.
Gauge: 13 sts = 2" (5 cm).

Mitten body: With dark wool, CO 54 sts. Join. Work in pattern until piece measures 2 ½" (6.5 cm). Begin normal thumb gore and work as charted for 20

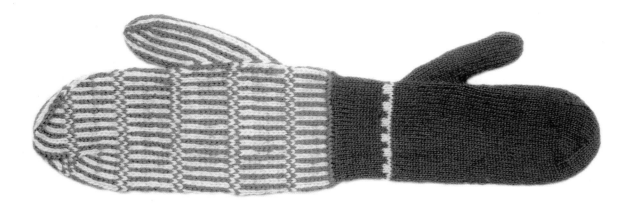

rnds—21 thumb sts. Place thumb sts on yarn length. Cont across rnd, CO 1 st over held thumb sts, and rejoin—54 sts. Cont in pattern until piece measures to tip of little finger. Work 3-point dec as charted. Draw up rem sts. *Thumb:* Place thumb sts on needles, pick up 3 sts along the CO st on the mitten body, and join—24 sts. Work even until piece measures to middle of thumbnail. Work 3-point dec as charted. Draw up rem sts.

INNER MITTEN
Materials: 2 oz (56.5 g) sport-weight wool; size 2 (2.75 mm) double-pointed needles.
Gauge: 15 sts = 2" (5 cm).

Mitten body and thumb: Pick up and knit 54 sts from the purl bumps on the Outer Mitten CO row. Work as for Outer Mitten, placing thumb gore in mirror position so that the inner thumb will tuck inside the outer thumb when the mitten is worn, and working the thumb before completing the body so that all loose yarn ends can be woven in and the stress point reinforced before access to the inside is lost. Add patterns and messages as desired.

Lined Mittens

Thumb Top

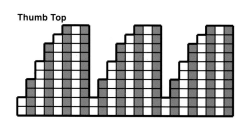

Thumb Gore

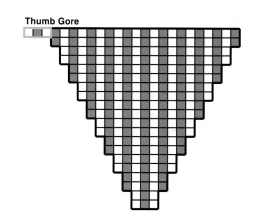

Lined Mittens

Mitten Body

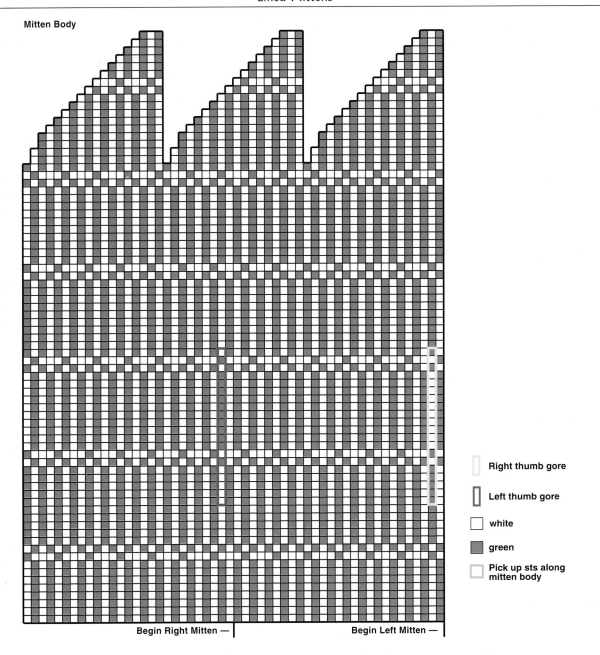

Right thumb gore

Left thumb gore

☐ white

▨ green

Pick up sts along mitten body

Begin Right Mitten —

Begin Left Mitten —

Double-Knit Mittens

Double-knit mittens are thick, comfortable, and completely reversible. Because air is trapped between the double-facing fabric, this type of mitten provides unsurpassed warmth. The two layers are knit simultaneously. Though the knitting proceeds somewhat slowly, it is worth the effort. These mittens are also well suited for pulling on over thinly knit gloves or mittens.

The double-knit technique can be used with any two-color "single-layer" pattern, but be aware that double-knitting may affect patterns in two ways: Tight gauges are difficult to achieve with double-knitting, even with small needles, and color patterns will be slightly broader when worked in double-knitting. Small repeating designs work well. Check your gauge with each new pattern.

Basic Rules of Double Knitting

(1) The needles will always hold stitches in this order: one knit stitch followed by one purl stitch. The knit stitch is the layer facing you. The following purl stitch belongs to the layer facing away from you.

(2) When working the yarn for the layer facing you, knit the stitch. When working the yarn for the layer facing away from you, purl the stitch.

(3) *Both* yarns are carried together and brought back and forth between every stitch. Yarns will lie forward when you are purling and in back when you are knitting.

4) A double-knitting chart shows only the pattern for the knit stitch, which is the fabric facing you. Its uncharted partner stitch is always purled with the opposite color yarn.

Casting On and Setting Up for Double-Knitting

With color A, loosely cast on enough stitches for one layer of knitting. With the same yarn, purl the next row. With the purl side facing, use another needle to pick up the purl bumps from the cast-on row. With color B, knit the first picked-up purl bump. Bring both yarns to the front, slip the first stitch already knit with color A onto the needle. Bring both yarns to the back and with color B, knit the next picked-up purl bump. Then bring both yarns to the front and slip the second stitch already knit. Continue in this manner until all picked-up stitches have been worked. There will be twice as many stitches as were cast on, and every knit stitch will have a purled partner. Divide the stitches evenly over three or four needles, keeping stitch partners together, and join into a round, being careful not to twist stitches.

Double-Knitting Increases

To increase, place both yarns in back. With the left needle, pick up and twist a loop from the yarns running between the fabric layers, and knit the loop. Bring both yarns forward and pick up and twist another loop, and purl it.

Double-Knitting Decreases

To decrease, slip the knit stitch off the left needle onto the right needle. Slip the purl stitch onto a holder. Place the first slipped stitch back onto the left needle, and knit two stitches together. Return the held purled stitch to the left needle, and purl two stitches together.

At the top of the body or thumb, the front-facing fabric is drawn up separately from the inner fabric layer as follows: Break off both yarns leaving 6-inch (15-cm) tails. To draw up the inner fabric layer, slide the first knit stitch onto a holding needle, then thread the tail of yarn used for the last purl stitch through the first purl stitch. Continue sliding the subsequent knit stitches onto a holding needle and threading the purl stitches onto the yarn length. Draw up stitches and fasten off. Draw up the outer fabric in the same way, using the other yarn tail.

Reading a Double-Knitting Chart

(1) Every square shown on a double-knitting chart represents two stitches—one knit stitch and its partner purl stitch. Only the stitches that will appear on the layer facing the knitter are shown.

(2) The first stitch of each pair is always a knit stitch made with the color indicated on the chart. Its partner purl stitch, always located to the left of the knit stitch, is made in the opposite color yarn.

3) A double-knitting chart is always read from right to left.

Houndstooth Double-Knit Mittens

The Scottish tweed houndstooth pattern adapts well to the double-knit technique. Please read the "Basic Rules of Double Knitting" above.

Finished Size: 8 ¾" (22 cm) around by 9" (23 cm) long.
Materials: 3 oz (85 g) each of two colors of worsted-weight wool (6 oz (170 g) total); size 2 (2.75 mm) double-pointed needles.
Gauge: 11 sts = 2" (5 cm).

Mitten body: With green, CO 48 sts and set up for double knitting as described on page 27. Divide the sts evenly over 3 needles, keeping partners tog, and join. On next rnd, work double-knitting inc in each st—96 sts (48 knit/purl pairs). Begin double-knitting, working pattern as charted for 16 rnds. On next rnd, begin side seam thumb gore and work as charted for 20 rnds—40 thumb sts (20 sts of each color). Place thumb sts on yarn length. Rejoin and cont double-knitting as charted until piece measures to tip of little finger. Work 4-point dec as charted. Draw up rem sts. *Thumb:* Place thumb sts on needles and join. Work as charted or until piece measures to middle of thumbnail. Work 3-point dec as charted. Draw up rem sts. *Side loop:* Finger-knit two 2-ft (62-cm) yarn lengths to make a 2" (5 cm) cord. (See page 18.) Attach cord to mitten cuff.

Houndstooth Double-Knit Mittens

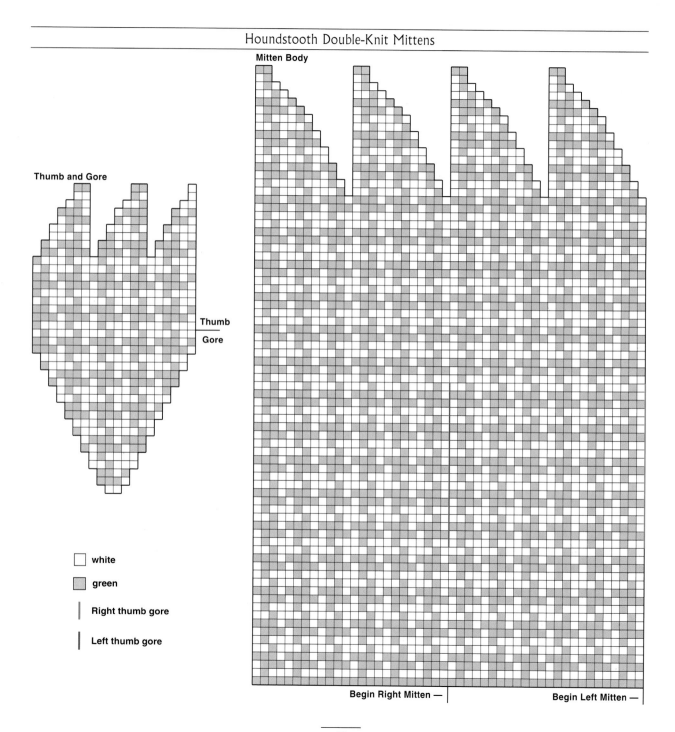

Mitten Body

Thumb and Gore

Thumb

Gore

☐ white

▨ green

▮ **Right thumb gore**

▮ **Left thumb gore**

Begin Right Mitten —

Begin Left Mitten —

Mittens from Europe

Denmark

Evidence of knitting in Scandinavia dates back to the early 1600s in Denmark. By the middle of the century, knitting had become an essential source of income. After the day's chores were finished, young and old would spend the evening at knitting parties. By the light of a whale-oil lamp, the knitters would discuss the day's events, sing sagas, and tell stories into the night. Yarn was wound onto dried goose windpipes filled with dried peas. The rattling of the peas assured all that work was being done.

Women's hands were never idle. They knit as they traveled to market or church and even as they ate. Some especially skilled women were reported to have knit, plied yarn, churned butter, and rocked the baby, all at the same time. Men also lent a hand knitting as they herded animals on foot or by horseback. Children learned to spin, card, and knit by the time they were five years old.

Danish sheep were said to be so small that a woman could carry two under each arm. The sheep shed their fleece naturally and children were sent "wool-gathering" through the moors.

Dog hair was often spun with the wool to strengthen the yarn, and folklore declared that dog hair would protect the wearer from gout. It certainly did make the garment prickly, and it did attract dogs. Because yarns blending wool and dog hair were water-repellent, they were particularly popular for fishermen's mittens.

Denmark is best known for the damask or brocade knitting used in the snug-fitting blouses that have become part of the national costume. The natural-color yarns used were dyed after the garment was completed: red for summer and feast days, green for spring and work days, and blue for winter and holiday wear.

Danish Hotpad

Denmark's damask knitting, worked in cotton to accentuate the rich texturing, makes an attractive hotpad.

Finished Size: 9" (23 cm) around by 7 ¾" (19.5 cm) long.

Materials: 2 oz (56.5 g) medium-weight cotton; size 2 (2.75 mm) double-pointed needles.

Gauge: 14 sts = 2" (5 cm).

Danish Hotpad

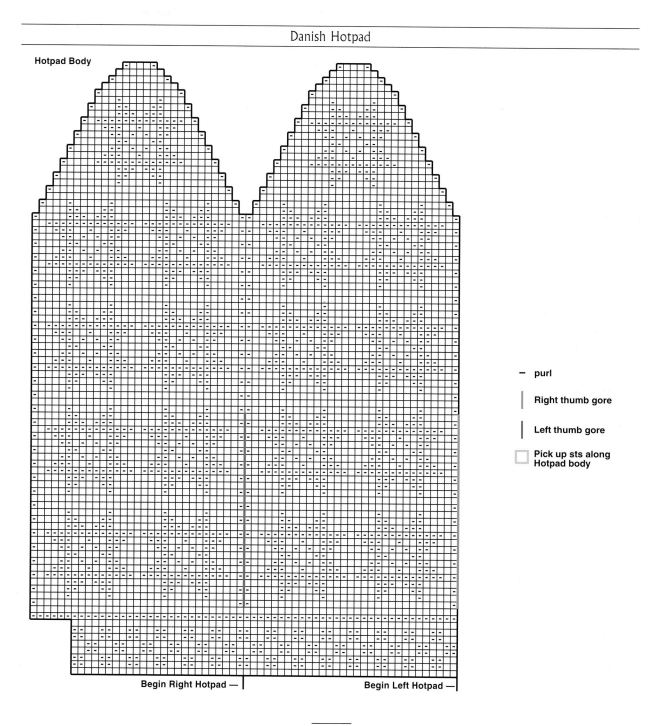

Hotpad Body

— purl

| Right thumb gore

| Left thumb gore

☐ Pick up sts along Hotpad body

Begin Right Hotpad —

Begin Left Hotpad —

Hotpad body: CO 56 sts. Join. Work as charted, inc 6 sts evenly spaced on 8th rnd—62 sts. On rnd 11, begin side seam thumb gore and work as charted for 28 rnds—24 thumb sts. Place thumb sts on yarn length. Rejoin and cont according to chart, working flat dec as shown. Draw up rem sts. **Thumb:** Place thumb sts on needles, pick up 2 sts along the hotpad body, and join—26 sts. Work even until piece measures to middle of thumbnail. Work 3-point dec as charted. Draw up rem sts. Finger-knit a 2" (5 cm) cord. (See page 18.) Attach cord to mitten.

Danish Fisherman's Mittens

Danish fishermen used "spear" mittens made with two thumbs. Because the thumb area was the first to wear out, mittens with an extra thumb lasted twice as long. The checkerboard pattern comes from early Jutland mittens.

Finished Size: 8" (20.5 cm) around by 7 ½" (19 cm) long, excluding ribbing.

Materials: 2 oz (56.5 g) brown worsted-weight wool; 2 oz (56.5 g) white worsted-weight wool; size 2 (2.75 mm) double-pointed needles.

Gauge: 16 sts = 2" (5 cm).

Danish Hotpad

Thumb Top

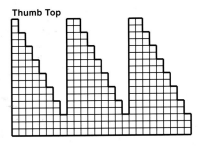

Thumb Gore

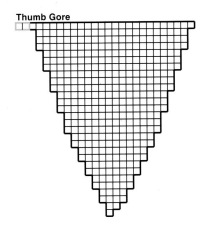

Danish Fisherman's Mittens

Thumb Top

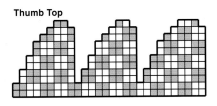

Thumb Gore

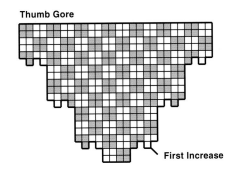

First Increase

Danish Fisherman's Mittens

Mittens knit with two thumbs last twice as long.
When one thumb wears out, simply flip the mitten over and use the other.

Danish Fisherman's Mittens

Mitten Body

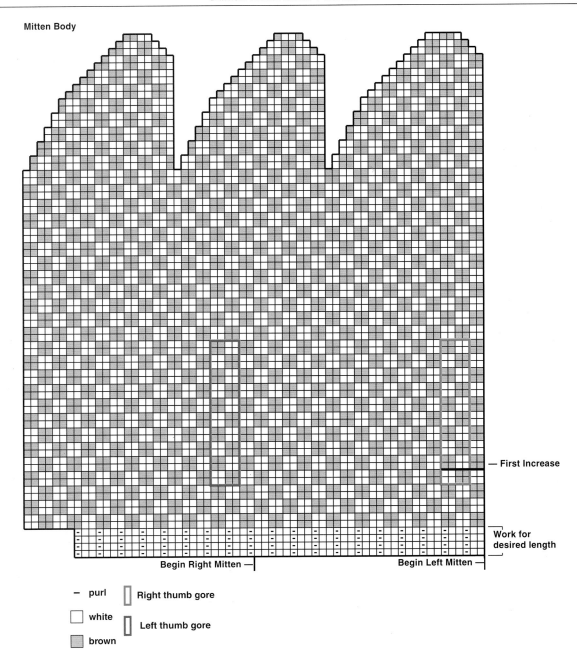

— First Increase

Work for desired length

Begin Right Mitten —

Begin Left Mitten —

- purl

☐ white

▨ brown

▯ Right thumb gore

▮ Left thumb gore

Mitten body: With brown, CO 57 sts. Join. Work 2x1 rib for desired length, then inc 7 sts evenly spaced—64 sts. Work as charted for 5 more rnds. On next rnd, begin normal thumb gore(s) and work as charted for 20 rnds—28 thumb sts. (To retain pattern sequence, work 4 incs over 2 rnds at both sides, then work 4 rnds even.) To make two-thumbed mittens, work thumb gores for both a right and left thumb on both mittens. Place thumb sts on yarn length. Rejoin and work even until piece measures to tip of little finger. Work 3-point dec as charted. Draw up rem sts. *Thumb:* Place thumb sts on needles and join. Work even until piece measures to middle of thumbnail. Work 3-point dec as charted. Draw up rem sts.

Sweden

The rich textile traditions of Sweden have been described as *folkligt*, meaning folksy, and demonstrate the practical improvisations that have directed the evolution of Swedish knitting. The craft dates back to the mid-seventeenth century, when men as well as women were expert knitters. Knitted items were important for family wear and for trade in the marketplace. Tenants paid for their room, board, and taxes with mittens.

Swedish wool textiles were often felted to increase warmth. In work wear, dog hair was spun with the wool for increased water-repellency. Rabbit hair was added to whiten and soften the yarn.

Over the years, superstitions grew around Swedish knitting. It was believed that garments with patterns winding counterclockwise would bring bad luck and prevent the wearer from entering heaven. It was also considered bad luck to knot together loose yarns. Garments knit by young maidens endowed the wearer with good luck and long life.

Gotland Island Mittens

The oldest knitting tradition in Scandinavia is reported to be from the island of Gotland, southeast of the Swedish mainland in the Baltic Sea. It was well situated for foreign trade, and the islanders used their knitting to barter for imported necessities. Gotland knitting was highly valued.

Spinning, carding, and dyeing were all traditionally done by women, who would gather to lighten their chore load with companionship. Although most of the knitting fell to the women, men and children were known to help.

Gotland Island Mittens

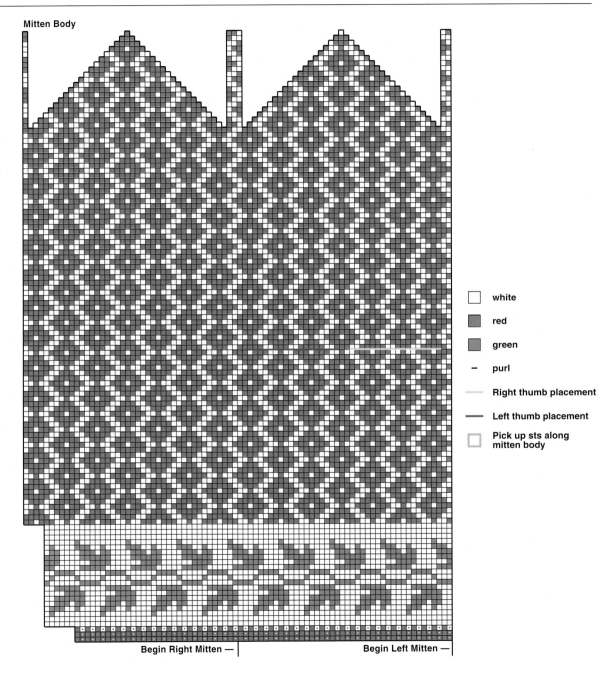

Mitten Body

white

red

green

- purl

Right thumb placement

Left thumb placement

Pick up sts along
mitten body

Begin Right Mitten —

Begin Left Mitten —

The patterns illustrate the knitters' close ties to nature, with wildflowers, vines, and ivies of the local meadows. Wedding stockings always included flowers to represent joy and vines (which grew hardily and readily after their roots established a firm foothold) to symbolize faithfulness. These stockings were made with the softest spring wool, spun finely and worked with intricate details. They were reputed to be so pliable that they could be rolled invisibly into the palm of a hand. For added durability, mittens were knit large and felted to size with soap,

water, and vigorous rubbing against a washboard. Long cuffs were preferred, some reaching to the elbows. Work wear was knit with heavier wool, to which cow hair was often added for strength and water-repellency.

Finished Size: 8" (20.5 cm) around by 10" (25.5 cm) long, including cuff.

Materials: 2 oz (56.5 g) red sport-weight wool; 1 ½ oz (42.5 g) white sport-weight wool; ½ oz (28.5 g) green sport-weight wool; contrasting waste yarn; size 1 (2.25 mm) double-pointed needles.

Gauge: 20 sts = 2" (5 cm).

Mitten body: With red, CO 74 sts. Join. Work 1x1 rib for 2 rnds, join white, and work 1x1 corrugated rib for 1 rnd, then inc 6 sts evenly spaced—80 sts, and work vine pattern as charted, inc 4 sts evenly spaced on last rnd—84 sts. Work even in pattern for 34 rnds. On next rnd, mark peasant thumb with contrasting waste yarn over 18 sts as shown. Work even until piece measures to top of little finger. Work flat dec as charted. Draw up rem sts. **Thumb:** Remove waste yarn, place thumb sts on needles, pick up 2 sts each side of picked-up sts, and join—40 sts. Work even as charted or until piece measures to middle of thumbnail. Work flat dec as charted. Draw up rem sts.

Gotland Island Mittens

Right Thumb

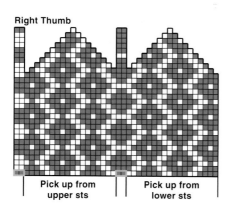

Pick up from upper sts   Pick up from lower sts

Left Thumb

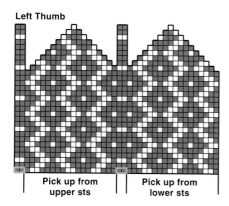

Pick up from upper sts   Pick up from lower sts

Lovikka Mittens

The first mittens from the Swedish area of Lovikka were knit in 1892. An innovative craftswoman who regularly knit for townspeople was commissioned by a woodsman to knit a pair of thick, long-wearing mittens. She spun and knit the mittens with extra-thick yarn to give them added warmth. The woodsman,

Lovikka Mittens

Mitten Body

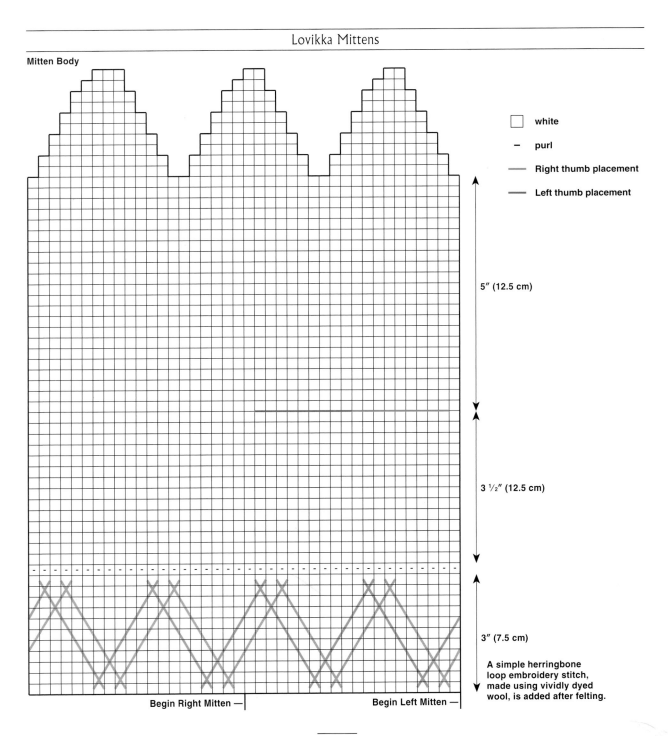

white

– purl

Right thumb placement

Left thumb placement

5″ (12.5 cm)

3 ½″ (12.5 cm)

3″ (7.5 cm)

A simple herringbone loop embroidery stitch, made using vividly dyed wool, is added after felting.

Begin Right Mitten —

Begin Left Mitten —

however, thought she had spoiled the wool. She took them home and felted them to her size. She then carded both the inside and outside of the mittens to raise the pile. This process created a solid fabric that was both soft and fluffy. This type of felted mitten became popular throughout the district, and was especially in demand among farmers who drove teams during the winter. The mittens were knit in bulky natural cream-colored wool. For color, the cuffs were embroidered with vivid patterns in wool.

Finished Size: 8 ½" (21.5 cm) around by 10" (25.5 cm) long, including cuff, after felting.

Materials: 4 ½ oz (127.5 g) bulky lopi; yarn for embroidery; contrasting waste yarn; size 7 (4.5 mm) double-pointed needles.

Gauge: 8 sts = 2" (5 cm).

Lovikka Mittens

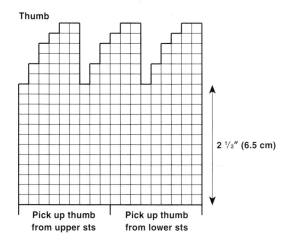

Thumb

2 ½" (6.5 cm)

Pick up thumb from upper sts   Pick up thumb from lower sts

Mitten body: CO 40 sts. Join. Knit 3" (7.5 cm), then purl 1 rnd for cuff. Knit even for 3 ½" (9 cm). With contrasting waste yarn, mark peasant thumb over 9 sts as shown. Work even until piece measures to top of the index finger. Work 3-point dec as charted. Draw up rem sts. **Thumb:** Remove waste yarn, place 18 thumb sts on needles, and join. Work even until piece measures to tip of thumb. Work 3-point dec as charted. Draw up rem sts.

Felt to size. (See Techniques, page 8.) Attach 4" (10-cm) braided cord at purled cuff rnd. Brush up pile. Embroider with contrasting yarn.

Mittens from Halland

From the heavily forested Halland area of Sweden comes the Ullard jersey worn by loggers in the nineteenth century. These sweaters were tightly knit and renowned for their warmth and wind resistance. The body was patterned in small diagonals and was framed by a small border. The wearer's initials and the date

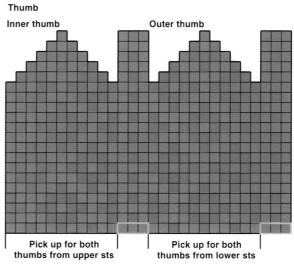

Mittens from Halland

Thumb
Inner thumb   Outer thumb

Pick up for both
thumbs from upper sts   Pick up for both
thumbs from lower sts

the sweater was made were often knit into the cuff or sweater body. Typically, the sweater was made with black and white wool, then felted to size and overdyed red.

These mittens incorporate the traditional patterns of Halland's lumberjack jerseys. The cuffs may be worked in corrugated ribbing or in stockinette stitch with a block for initials. (See chart.)

Finished Size: 8 ¹/₂" (21.5 cm) around by 10" (25.5 cm) long.

Materials: 2 oz (56.5 g) red worsted-weight wool; 1 ¹/₂ oz (42.5 g) black worsted-weight wool; contrasting waste yarn; size 3 (3.25 mm) double-pointed needles.

Gauge: 13 sts = 2" (5 cm).

Mitten body: With black, CO 50 sts. Join. **Cuff option:** Work 1x1 corrugated rib alternating black and red for 18 rnds. **Cuff option:** Work 1x1 corrugated rib for 3 rnds, then on next rnd, insert initials into cuff chart, adjusting cuff stitch count between 50 and 53 sts as needed for initials. Then for both options, inc 6 sts evenly spaced—56 sts. Cont as charted for 19 rnds. On next rnd, with contrasting waste yarn, mark peasant thumb over 11 sts as shown. Cont as charted until piece measures to top of little finger. Work flat dec as charted. Draw up rem sts. **Thumb:** Remove waste yarn, place thumb sts on needles, pick up 3 sts each side of picked-up sts, and join—28 sts. Work even as charted or until piece measures to middle of thumbnail. Work flat dec as charted. Draw up rem sts.

Mittens from Halland

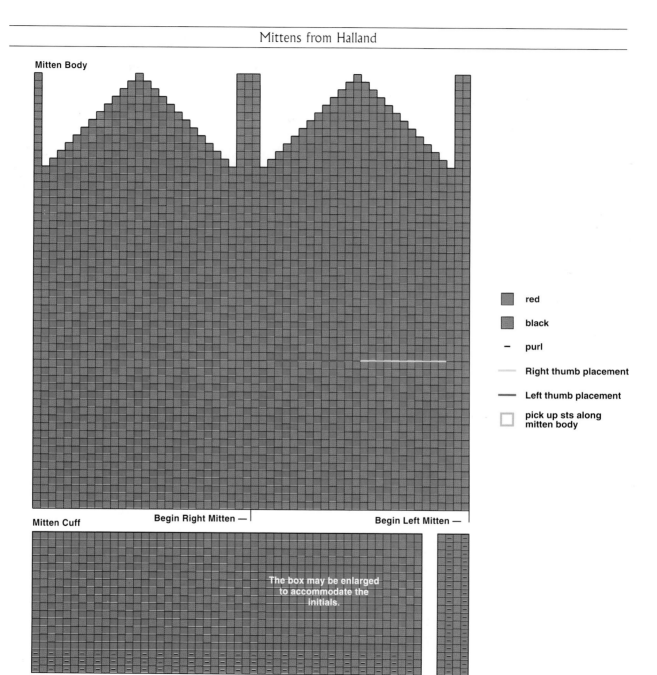

Mitten Body

Mitten Cuff

Begin Right Mitten —

Begin Left Mitten —

The box may be enlarged
to accommodate the
initials.

Right cuff | **Left cuff**

red

black

— purl

Right thumb placement

Left thumb placement

□ pick up sts along
mitten body

Bohus Stickning

Knitted garments from the Bohus Stickning workshop in Sweden are recognizable by their unique color changes along with combinations of knit and purl stitches.

Bohus Stickning

Bohus *Stickning*, or knitting, is famous for its combination of color with fabric texture. Its unique beauty involves many color changes along with a combination of knit and purl stitches. This technique began in 1939 as a home-based industry for winter relief work in Sweden's southern Bohus Province. To ease the effects of unemployment on the families of the local stonecutters, Emma Jacobsson, wife of the governor, formed a cooperative. The wives of unemployed stonecutters met at monthly teas to share techniques and learn new patterns. The cooperative was disbanded in 1969.

The pattern for these mittens was adapted from the yoke of a Bohus Stickning sweater.

Finished Size: 8 ¼" (21 cm) around by 8" (20.5 cm) long, excluding cuff.

Materials: 3 oz (85 g) cream worsted-weight wool; ½ oz (14 g) each of 3 shades purple worsted-weight wool; size 4 (3.5 mm) double-pointed needles.

Gauge: 12 sts = 2" (5 cm).

Mitten body: With cream, CO 45 sts. Join. Work 2x1 rib for desired length, then change to body pattern and inc 5 sts evenly spaced—50 sts. Work as charted for 2 more rnds. On the next rnd, begin normal thumb gore and work as charted for 20 rnds—20 sts. Place thumb sts on yarn length. Cont across rnd, CO 1 st over held thumb sts, and rejoin—50 sts. Work even until piece measures to top of little finger. Work 3-point dec as charted. Draw up rem sts.

Thumb: Place thumb sts on needles and join. Work as charted or until piece measures to middle of thumbnail. Work 3-point dec as charted. Draw up rem sts.

Bohus Stickning Mittens

Right Thumb

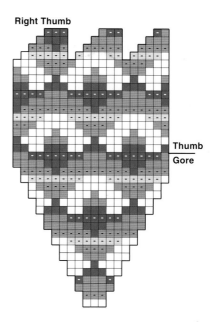

Thumb
Gore

Left Thumb

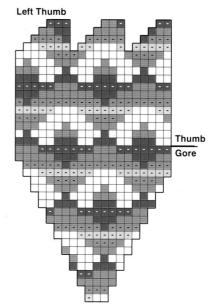

Thumb
Gore

Bohus Stickning Mittens

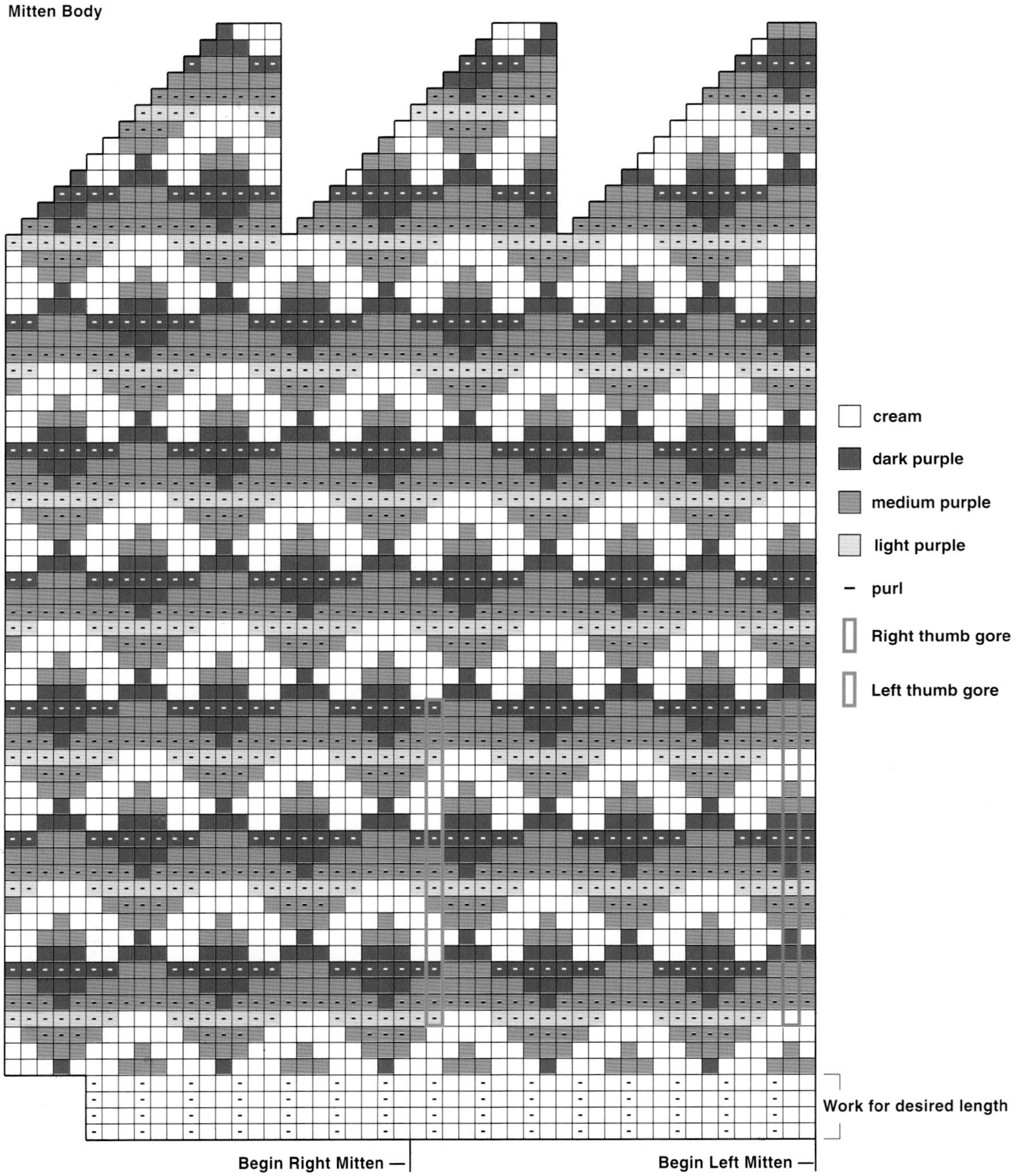

Mitten Body

☐	cream
■	dark purple
▨	medium purple
☐	light purple
–	purl
▯	Right thumb gore
▯	Left thumb gore

Work for desired length

Begin Right Mitten —| Begin Left Mitten —|

Norway

Norway, whose coastlines reach from the North Sea in the south to the Barents Sea in the north, is renowned for the dramatic beauty of its long, cold winters. Knitting dates to the 1500s and is deeply ingrained in Norwegian culture.

Children became skillful knitters at an early age, and entire families would knit during times of crisis or unemployment. Knitted goods were used in day-to-day bartering at the marketplace and as payment for room and board. When visiting, women would bring their knitting—they were rarely seen without yarn and needles. Some women were reported to knit so quickly that they could complete a pair of mittens on their way to market, stop at a farm on the way home to wash them, and hang them on their market baskets to dry.

Girls spent much of their time knitting mittens for their hope chests. A bride was expected to give a pair of mittens to every man who attended her wedding. With the help of friends and family, a maiden of marriageable age would have as many as one hundred pairs of mittens in her bridal loft. Most were worked in such fine wool that the pattern on the back of a mitten could fill an entire sweater if knit with the thicker wool and larger needles typically used today.

Garments intended for sailors or miners were usually knit with yarn spun from a combination of wool and human, goat, or cow hair for added strength.

Because the first part of a mitten to wear out was the thumb, some fisherman mittens were knit with two thumbs. The extra thumb was tucked inside the mitten. Work mittens were knit oversized then felted to fit. In the felting process, codfish gall bladders were stuffed inside the mittens and popped. The bladder's contents were thought to cleanse and strengthen the wool.

Setesdal Mittens

Setesdal is a valley district in the south of Norway. It is the home of the *luskofte*, or lice jacket, named for the flecked pattern in the body of the sweater. These striking sweaters were originally considered

Setesdal Mittens

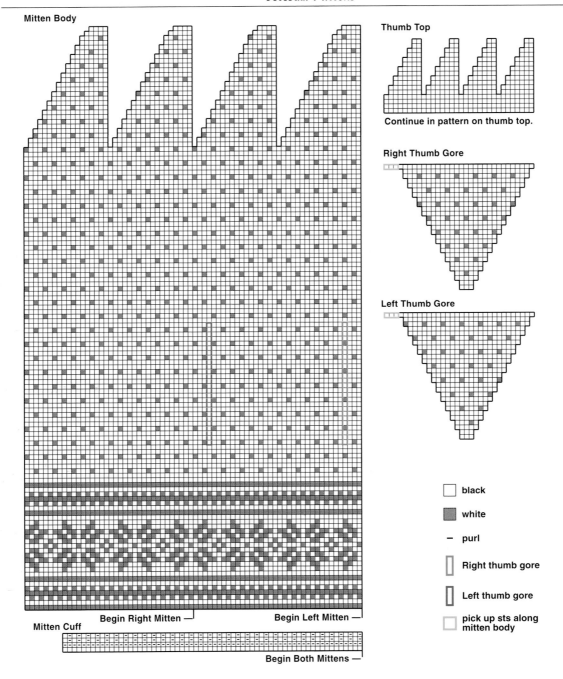

Mitten Body

Thumb Top

Continue in pattern on thumb top.

Right Thumb Gore

Left Thumb Gore

Begin Right Mitten —

Begin Left Mitten —

Mitten Cuff

Begin Both Mittens —

☐ black

▨ white

– purl

▯ Right thumb gore

▮ Left thumb gore

▢ pick up sts along mitten body

peasant wear for men but have become the unofficial national sweater for both men and women. They are knit in worsted-weight wool of white on black at a tight gauge, making a firm, dense fabric.

Finished Size: 8" (20.5 cm) around by 10" (25.5 cm) long.
Materials: 4 oz (113.5 g) black worsted-weight wool; 1 oz (28.5 g) white worsted-weight wool; size 0 (2 mm) double-pointed needles.
Gauge: 18 sts = 2" (5 cm).

Mitten body: With black, CO 64 sts. Join. Knit 1 rnd, purl 1 rnd. Work 1x1 rib for 2 rnds, then change to body pattern and inc 8 sts evenly spaced—72 sts. Work as charted to beg of thumb gore. Work normal thumb gore as charted for 27 rnds—29 thumb sts. Place thumb sts on yarn length. Cont across rnd, CO 1 st over held thumb sts, and rejoin—72 sts. Work even until piece measures to tip of little finger. Work 4-point dec as charted. Draw up rem sts.
Thumb: Place thumb sts on needles, pick up 3 sts along the mitten body, and join—32 sts. Work even until piece measures to middle of thumbnail. Work 4-point dec as charted. Draw up rem sts.

Selbu Mittens

Norway's oldest knitting tradition is two-stranded knitting with both strands from the same ball of yarn. As history records, it was a creative young knitter in the Selbu, a small northerly district, who first tried using two contrasting color yarns in her mittens. She wore her mittens to church and they became an instant hit. Among the many patterns that later developed, the favorite was the *sjenn-rosa* or eight-petaled rose, which we know as the Norwegian star.

Selbu knitters are also famous for their moose, reindeer, and hand-holding dancers motifs, worked in high-contrast colors such as white on black.

Finished Size: 8 1/2" (21.5 cm) around by 7 1/2" (19 cm) long, excluding cuff.
Materials: 2 1/2 oz (71 g) navy worsted-weight wool; 2 oz (56.5 g) white worsted-weight wool; contrasting waste yarn; size 3 (3.25 mm) double-pointed needles.
Gauge: 14 sts = 2" (5 cm).

Selbu Mittens

Mitten Body

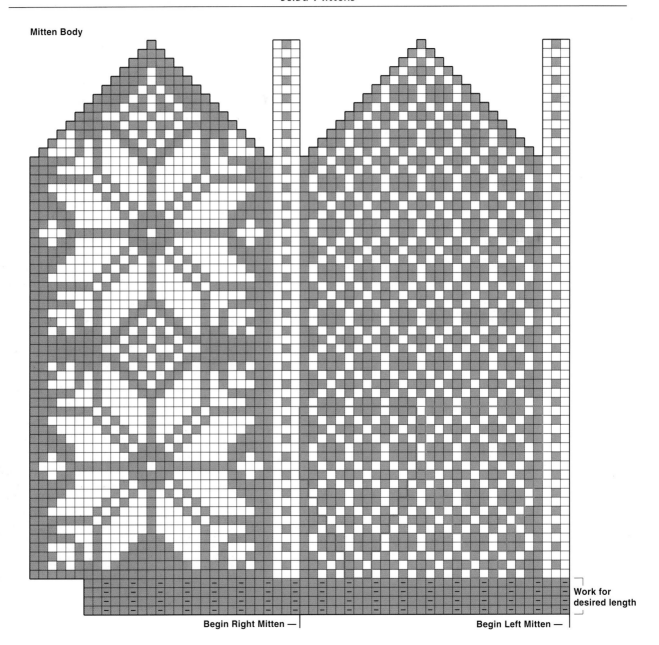

Begin Right Mitten —

Begin Left Mitten —

Work for desired length

Selbu Mittens

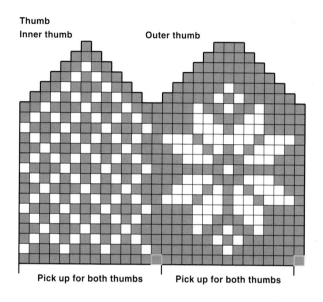

Thumb
Inner thumb | Outer thumb

Pick up for both thumbs | Pick up for both thumbs

Thumb Gore

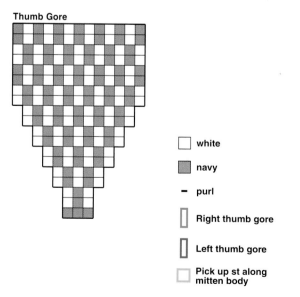

☐ white

■ navy

– purl

▯ Right thumb gore

▮ Left thumb gore

☐ Pick up st along
mitten body

Mitten body: With navy, CO 54 sts. Join. Work 2x1 rib for desired length. On next rnd, begin body patterning, inc 6 sts evenly spaced—60 sts, and beg Norwegian thumb gore as charted for 19 rnds. (Work the charted thumb gore pattern instead of the palm pattern.) On next rnd, with contrasting waste yarn, mark peasant thumb over 13 sts as shown. Cont as charted until piece measures to tip of little finger. Work flat dec as charted. Draw up rem sts. **Thumb:** Remove waste yarn, place thumb sts on needles, pick up 1 st each side, and join—28 sts. Work as charted or until piece measures to middle of thumbnail. Work flat dec as charted. Draw up rem sts.

Fana Mittens

During the eighteenth and early nineteenth centuries, Norway's Fana region was a land of hard-working farmers. Sweaters for farmhands were knit with

Fana Mittens

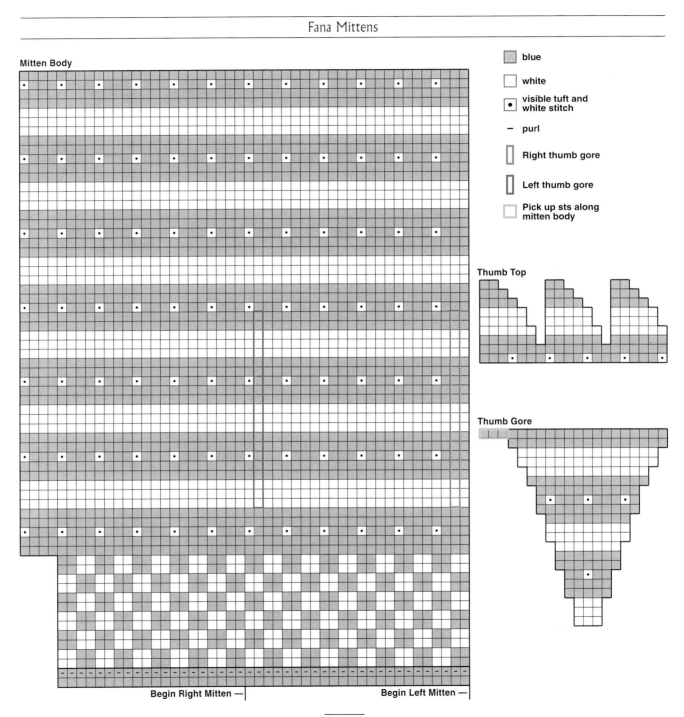

Mitten Body

	blue
	white
●	visible tuft and white stitch
–	purl
	Right thumb gore
	Left thumb gore
	Pick up sts along mitten body

Thumb Top

Thumb Gore

Begin Right Mitten —| Begin Left Mitten —|

To tuft a mitten

You can add thickness and warmth to a pair of mittens by knitting in tufts of unspun wool. Each tuft is a 5" (12.5-cm) length of combed wool which, ideally, contains lanolin. After it's given a twist in the middle, the wool tuft should be similar in thickness to the yarn being used. The tufts can be invisible on the mitten surface or worked as part of the color pattern. They should be placed every 4 to 6 stitches per row and worked every 4 to 8 rounds.

To work a tuft that will be invisible on the outside of the mitten, twist the tuft in the middle, place it over the left needle, insert right needle into next stitch, and knit it together with the tuft. On the next round, give the tuft a tug to set it in

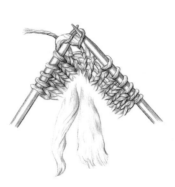

place. With the mitten's first wearing, spread out the tuft ends for even matting.

To work a tuft that will be visible as part of the color pattern, insert the right needle through the stitch below the first stitch on the left needle, place the twisted tuft over the top of the right needle and pull it through to the front of the work, then knit the stitch on the needle.

Pass the tufted yarn up and over the stitch just made.

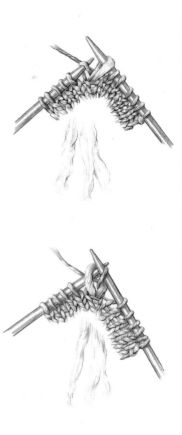

Fana Mittens

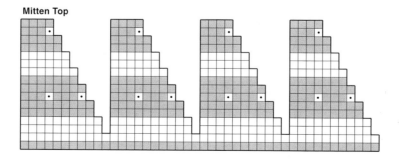

Mitten Top

blue and white flecked stripes and edged with a checkerboard pattern. In some areas of Norway, this sweater pattern became a symbol for peace during World War I.

A northern European technique of lining a mitten or hat with wool, called tufting, lends itself to this mitten. This warm, insulating lining dates back to hats of the late eighteenth century in Denmark and other Scandinavian countries. The brims were fashionably turned up to reveal the white fluffy lining. This idea is cheaply imitated today in the hat Santa Claus wears. Lengths of contrasting yarn or tufts of combed, unspun wool are periodically stitched in. The outside of the mitten is a pattern which the Finnish call *linnunsilmid* or bird's-eyes. Inside the mitten the yarn ends hang loose, creating a warm, rug-like lining. Because the yarn lengths are left loose inside the mitten, there are no yarns to be carried as you knit.

Finished Size: 9 ½" (24 cm) around by 10 ½" (26.5 cm) long, including cuff.
Materials: 2 oz. (57g) each of blue and white worsted-weight wool; tufts of unspun wool; size 4 (3.5 mm) double-pointed needles.
Gauge: 10 sts = 2" (5 cm).

Mitten body: With blue, CO 44 sts. Join. Purl 1 rnd. Work checkerboard pattern as charted, then beg striped pattern, inc 4 sts evenly spaced on first rnd—48 sts, and working visible tufts as charted. On 6th rnd, begin normal thumb gore and work as charted for 21 rnds—17 thumb sts. Place thumb sts on yarn length. Cont across rnd, CO 1 st over held thumb sts, and rejoin—48 sts. Cont as charted or until piece measures to tip of little finger. Work 4-point dec as charted. Draw up rem sts. **Thumb:** Place thumb sts

on needles, pick up 3 sts along mitten body, and join—20 sts. Work even until piece measures to middle of thumbnail. Work 3-point dec as charted. Draw up rem sts.

Finland

Finland is a land of thousands of lakes and swamps and vast tracts of timberland. More than a third of the country lies north of the Arctic Circle, and its winter months are cold and dark. People lived by farming, mining, logging, and seal hunting.

Finnish knitting was known for being warm and practical, and it was an essential part of folk costumes and customs. Handknit sweaters were traditional gifts of affection, given as an engagement present or as gifts of appreciation to teachers or midwives.

Knitting parties were an important social event. First, the young women would gather. After lingering a bit, the men would join them, and some would knit garters. The gatherings were lighthearted and filled with stories, jokes, and laughter.

A family's wealth and a bride's worth were judged by the quality and quantity of the textiles owned. Their goods, including mittens, were displayed in the family's summer sleeping lofts and a prospective suitor paying an evening visit could see what treasures his sweetheart's dowry contained.

During the eighteenth century, knitting became an important source of income for many families. Finland's famous master knitters would sit in a circle with knees touching, working together around the body of a sweater. Knitting became such a phenomenon in the southern city of Nadendad that officials forbade knitting in public places, declaring it a shameful activity that should not be done outside the home.

Thick and colorful Finnish mittens were knit for practicality and beauty. In the dead of winter, large skin mittens were worn over knitted wool ones. Finnish knitters enjoyed colors and patterns of high contrast: bold red, blue, and green patterns on a white or black background.

This mitten includes a collection of Finnish patterns from mittens knit in Tjock.

Finnish Mittens

Finished Size: 8 ½" (21.5 cm) around by 8 ¾" (22 cm) long, including cuff.

Materials: 2 ½ oz (71 g) white or black worsted-weight wool (background); 2 oz (56.5 g) total maroon, yellow, red, blue, light green, orange worsted-weight wool (motifs); contrasting waste yarn; size 2 (2.75 mm) double-pointed needles.

Gauge: 16 sts = 2" (5 cm).

Mitten body: With background color, CO 60 sts. Join. Work 1x1 rib for 9 rnds, then change to St st and inc 10 sts evenly spaced—70 sts. Work as charted for 26 more rnds. On next rnd, with contrasting waste yarn, mark peasant thumb over 14 sts as shown. Cont as charted or until piece measures to tip of little finger. Work flat dec as charted. Graft rem 18 sts with Kitchener st. **Thumb:** Remove waste yarn, place

Finnish Mittens

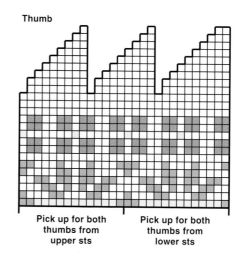

Thumb

Pick up for both thumbs from upper sts

Pick up for both thumbs from lower sts

Finnish Mittens

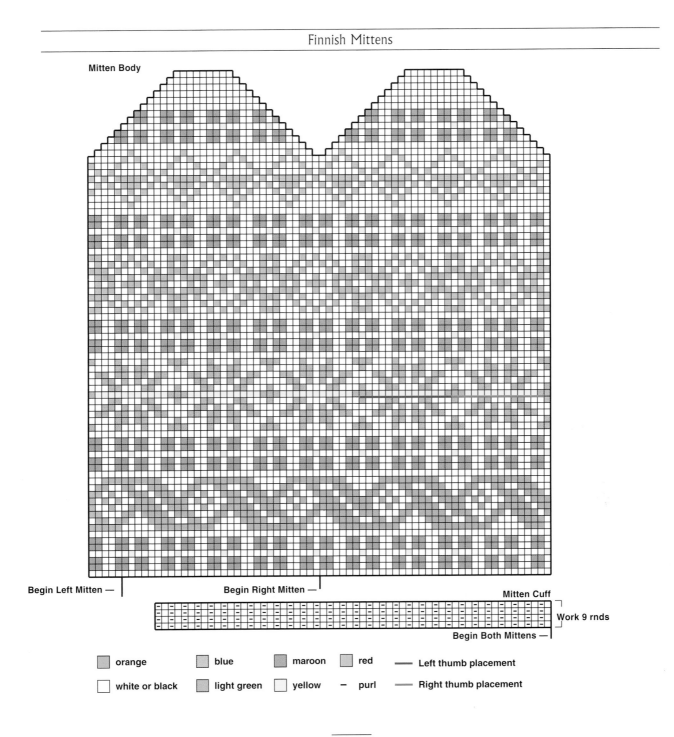

Mitten Body

Begin Left Mitten —

Begin Right Mitten —

Mitten Cuff

Work 9 rnds

Begin Both Mittens —

| | orange | | blue | | maroon | | red | — Left thumb placement |
| | white or black | | light green | | yellow | − purl | — Right thumb placement |

thumb sts on needles, and join—28 sts. Work as charted or until piece measures to middle of thumbnail. Work 3-point dec as charted. Draw up rem sts.

Lapland

Lapland, the land of the midnight sun, encompasses sections of Norway, Sweden, Finland, and Russia that lie north of the Arctic circle. It is the traditional home of semi-nomadic reindeer herdsmen known as Lapps. Winters are long, dark, and bitterly cold. The winter landscape is so closely tied to the Lapps' daily lives that their language contains more than twenty terms to describe snow.

Before knitting came to Lapland, Lapps stuffed fur mittens and boots with warm, soft hay. With the arrival of knitting, they made colorful mittens to brighten the snowy landscape, adding cords and tassels for identification and for hanging.

Mittens from Lapland

Finished Size: 8 ½" (21.5 cm) around by 10 ¾" (27.5 cm) long.

Materials: 2 oz (56.5 g) red worsted-weight wool; 2 oz (56.5 g) white worsted-weight wool; ½ oz (14 g) blue worsted-weight wool; contrasting waste yarn; size 2 (2.75 mm) double-pointed needles.

Gauge: 13 sts = 2" (5 cm).

Mitten body: With white and red and using 2-color CO with white over the thumb and red over the index finger (see Techniques, page 10), CO 52 sts. Join. Plait 3 rnds (see Techniques, page 11) as follows: *Rnd 1:* With both yarns forward, *p1 white, p1 red, bringing the color to be used *over* the color not used; rep from *. *Rnd 2:* With both yarns forward, *p1 white, p1 red, bringing the color to be used

under the color not used; rep from *. *Rnd 3:* Join blue (drop red) and with both yarns forward, *p1 white, p1 light blue, bringing the color to be used *over* the color not used; rep from *. Work as charted for 36 more rnds. On next rnd, with contrasting waste yarn, mark peasant thumb over 10 sts as shown. Cont as charted or until piece measures to tip of little finger. Work flat dec as charted. Draw up rem sts. **Thumb:** Remove waste yarn, place 20 thumb sts on needles, pick up 2 sts each side, and join—24 sts. Work as charted or until piece measures to middle of thumbnail. Work flat dec as charted. Draw up rem sts.

Attach a finger-knit cord and tassel to the plaited cuff. (See page 18.)

To make a tassel: Loop yarn around a stiff piece of cardboard that is the desired tassel length. Tie one end of the loops with a piece of yarn; this will be used

---

Mittens from Lapland

Thumb

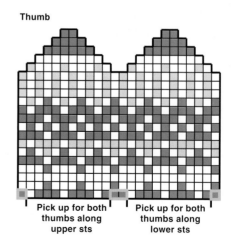

Pick up for both
thumbs along
upper sts

Pick up for both
thumbs along
lower sts

Mittens from Lapland

Lapps knit colorful mittens to brighten dark, snowy winters.

Mittens from Lapland

Mitten Body

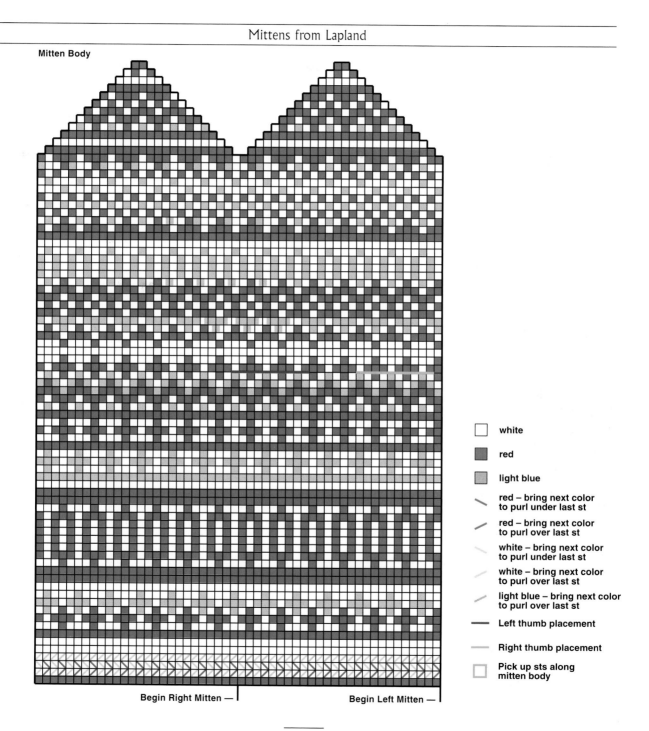

white

red

light blue

red – bring next color
to purl under last st

red – bring next color
to purl over last st

white – bring next color
to purl under last st

white – bring next color
to purl over last st

light blue – bring next color
to purl over last st

Left thumb placement

Right thumb placement

Pick up sts along
mitten body

Begin Right Mitten —

Begin Left Mitten —

to attach the tassel to the cord. Slip the loops off the cardboard and tie another piece of yarn around the loops near the top. Cut ends neatly to desired length.

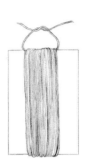 

The Baltics

The Baltic countries of Latvia, Estonia, and Lithuania line the heavily forested eastern shore of the Baltic Sea. Men harvested fish, eels, seals, and sprat while women tended to the crops and home. When these chores were finished the women took up their knitting.

Baltic knitting is famous for its intricately detailed patterns from the region's mythology. Human and animal motifs, believed to bring bad luck, were avoided. Surrounded by the stark colors of long, dark winters, knitters chose boldly dyed yarns of red, blue, yellow, and green.

Mittens played an important role in traditions of courtship and marriage in the Baltics, particularly in Latvia. A maiden's worth was measured in part by her skill in knitting and by the number of mittens she had made. When a young woman accepted a marriage proposal, she sent her suitor a pair of mittens. He would drape them over his belt as a sign that he was committed. On the wedding day, the couple's relatives and all who helped with the marriage were presented with a pair of mittens or socks. The newlyweds ate the marriage feast with mittened hands, and the marriage threshold could be crossed only after a pair of mittens had been laid down. A proper marriage required a hundred or more pairs of mittens.

Baltic Mittens

This is just one example of the countless skillfully crafted mittens that have played a major part in Baltic cultures for centuries.

Krisjanis Barons collected Latvian folk songs called *dainas* in the late nineteenth century that demonstrate

Baltic Mittens

Mitten Body

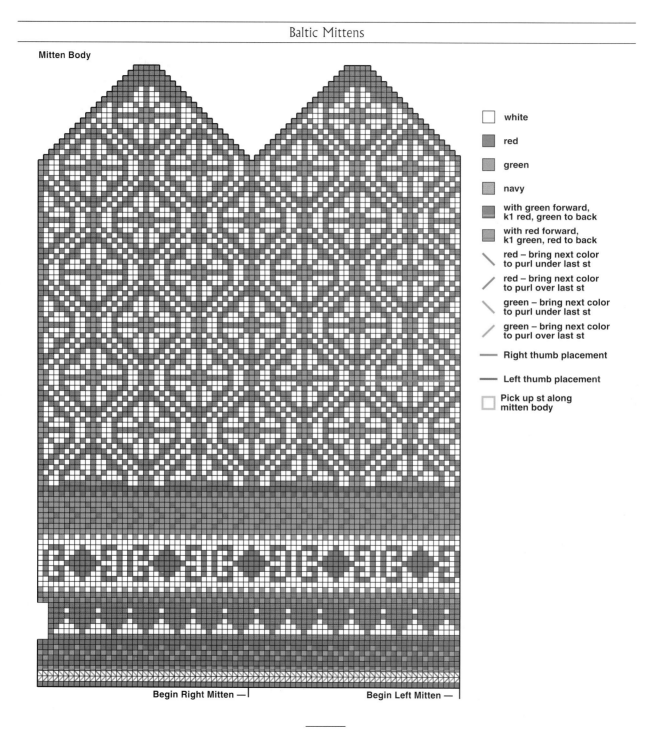

white

red

green

navy

with green forward,
k1 red, green to back

with red forward,
k1 green, red to back

red – bring next color
to purl under last st

red – bring next color
to purl over last st

green – bring next color
to purl under last st

green – bring next color
to purl over last st

Right thumb placement

Left thumb placement

Pick up st along
mitten body

Begin Right Mitten —|

Begin Left Mitten —|

the mittens' honored place in Latvia's culture. This is one of the hundreds of dainas that refers to knitting.

Good evening, maiden's mother
As you see my hands are freezing;
All the while my mitten knitter
Snugly in your room is sitting.

Finished Size: 8" (20.5 cm) around by 11 ¼" (28.5 cm) long.

Materials: 1 ½ oz (42.5 g) navy sport-weight wool; 1 ½ oz (42.5 g) white sport-weight wool; ½ oz (14 g) green sport-weight wool; ½ oz (14 g) red sport-weight wool; contrasting waste yarn; size 1 (2.25 mm) double-pointed needle.

Gauge: 19 sts = 2" (5 cm).

Mitten body: With red and green and using 2-color CO with green over the thumb and red over the index finger (see Techniques, page 10), CO 80 sts. Join. Plait 2 rnds (see Techniques, page 11) as follows: *Rnd 1:* With both yarns forward, *p1 green, p1 red, bringing the color to be used *over* the color not used; rep from *. *Rnd 2:* With both yarns forward, *p1 red, p1 green, bringing the color to be used *under* the color not used; rep from *. *Rnd 3:* *With green forward and red in back, k1 red, with green in back and red forward, k1 green; rep from *. Work as charted for 5 rnds, dec 2 sts evenly on 5th rnd—78 sts. Work as charted for 6 more rnds, then inc 2 sts evenly—80 sts. Cont as charted to thumb placement (54 rnds total above plaiting). On next rnd, with contrasting waste yarn, mark peasant thumb over 17 sts as shown. Cont as charted or until piece measures to tip of little finger. Work flat dec as charted. Draw up rem sts. ***Thumb:*** Remove waste yarn, place 34 thumb sts on needles, pick up 1 st each side, and join—36 sts. Work as charted or until piece measures to middle of thumbnail. Work flat dec as charted. Draw up rem sts.

The Island of Runo

In the Baltic Sea near Latvia, Lithuania, and Estonia lie numerous islands. Maritime tradition has it that the more remote the island from the mainland, the higher the skills of its craftspeople. The island of Runo, off the coast of Estonia, was no exception. Life was hard and livelihoods were wrenched from the land and sea. Women had the time-consuming

---

Baltic Mittens

Thumb

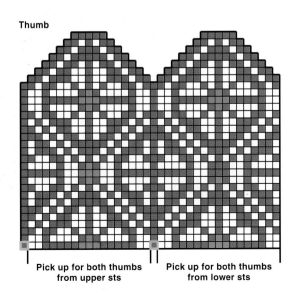

Pick up for both thumbs from upper sts　　　**Pick up for both thumbs from lower sts**

chore of making all the family clothing by hand, and any spare time was filled with knitting. Runo's inhabitants knit as they walked to market or the fields, when they went visiting, or when they gathered around the fire at day's end.

The Island of Runo is home to a unique technique of weaving in a pattern while knitting. This technique, which has been worked into stockings for more than five centuries, gives a padded look and creates a more striking contrast than a knitted-in pattern.

Mittens from the Island of Runo

These mittens incorporate the unique weaving traditions of the Island of Runo. Weaving is done with a contrasting yarn of the same weight or slightly heavier than the main yarn. This contrasting yarn is neither knit nor purled, but simply carried across the front of the work as indicated by the chart. Separate lengths of yarn are used for each round, and the ends are woven in later.

When the chart indicates a woven stitch (or stitches), bring the weaving yarn forward. Work the

Mittens from the Island of Runo

Thumb Top

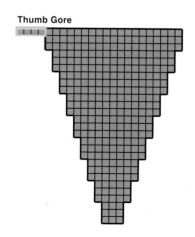

Thumb Gore

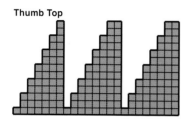

Mittens from the Island of Runo

Mitten Body

	white
	navy
	white woven st
−	purl
	Right thumb gore
	Left thumb gore
	Pickup sts along mitten body

Note: Place motif on back of hand only

Begin Right Mitten —| Begin Left Mitten —|

designated number of stitches in the background color, then bring the contrasting yarn to the back between needle tips and carry it in the back of work as usual.

Finished Size: 8 ½" (21.5 cm) around by 9 ½" (24 cm) long, including cuff.
Materials: 4 oz (113.5 g) navy worsted-weight wool; ½ oz (14 g) white worsted-weight wool; size 2 (2.75 mm) double-pointed needles.
Gauge: 14 sts = 2" (5 cm).

Mitten body: With white, CO 60 sts. Join. Work 2x2 rib for 8 rnds (1" (2.5 cm)). Work as charted for 2 rnds, then inc 2 sts evenly spaced—62 sts. Work even for 6 more rnds. On next rnd, begin normal thumb gore and work for 27 rnds as charted—19 thumb sts. Place thumb sts on yarn length. Cont across rnd, CO 1 st over held thumb sts, and rejoin— 62 sts. Cont as charted or until piece measures to tip of little finger. Work flat dec as charted. Graft rem 18 sts with Kitchener st. *Thumb:* Place thumb sts on needles, pick up 4 sts along the mitten body, and join—23 sts. Work even until piece measures to middle of thumbnail. Work 3-point dec as charted. Draw up rem sts.

Iceland

Iceland is a North Atlantic island that just skirts the Arctic Circle. Winters are cold, wet, and windy. Iceland's woolen goods, designed to protect against the elements, are renowned for their heavyweight warmth.

Both women and men helped clothe their families in Iceland. Men carded and combed the wool, while women did most of the spinning. Both men and women

knit. Long winter evenings found everyone gathered around the hearth knitting while old sagas were read. It was there that most of the children's education took place. Icelanders were skilled craftspeople and rapid knitters. Children were expected to knit two pairs of mittens in a week, while maidservants were to knit a pair of long stockings in a day or two sweaters a week.

Wool was an important Icelandic commodity and at one time served as its legal currency. Knitted garments were the most commonly traded item in the 1600s, and tenants of church-owned farms paid part of their rent with handknit socks. Folklore had it that everyone must have newly knit garments for Christmas or risk being eaten by the large and dangerous Christmas cat described in ancient sagas.

Sheep were brought to Iceland by Viking settlers in the ninth century. In response to centuries of hostile Icelandic weather, the sheep developed unique fleeces with an outer coat of long, coarse hair for protection from wet and cold over a fine, soft inner coat for insulation. Icelandic yarn is spun with a combination of both coats. For many centuries, Icelandic yarn was tightly spun like other European yarns. Now famous, *lopi* yarn was not used until the 1920s. Legend has it that a farmer's wife, in a great hurry to knit a scarf for her husband, used fleece that had been combed and teased, but not yet properly spun. The resulting scarf was pleasing, soft, and warm, and a new tradition had begun.

Early Icelandic knitters did little dyeing, preferring the natural color of wool. Patterns were geometric and repetitive. Large outer mittens made of coarser yarn were worn over fine, pliable mittens or gloves. Thumbs, at times two per mitten, were commonly worked on very fine needles to make them warmer and longer-lasting. Mittens worn by sailors usually included a cross motif to protect them at sea.

North Iceland Mittens

This mitten comes from northern Iceland, where rolled ribbon and arrowhead patterns were common.

Finished Size: 8" (20.5 cm) around by 7 ¾" (19.5 cm) long, excluding cuff.

Materials: 3 oz (85 g) natural light lopi; 1 oz (28.5 g) black light lopi; ½ oz (14 g) red light lopi; contrasting waste yarn; size 2 (2.75 mm) double-pointed needles.

Gauge: 13 sts = 2" (5 cm).

Mitten body: With natural, CO 48 sts. Join. Work 2x1 rib for desired length, then inc 4 sts on next rnd—52 sts. Work as charted for 16 more rnds. On next rnd, with contrasting waste yarn, mark peasant thumb over 10 sts as shown. Cont as charted or until piece measures to the tip of the little finger. Work flat dec as charted. Draw up rem sts. **Thumb:** Remove waste yarn, place 20 thumb sts on needles, pick up 1 st each side, and join—22 sts. Work even in St st until piece measures to middle of thumbnail. Work 3-point dec as charted. Draw up rem sts.

North Iceland Mittens

Thumb Top

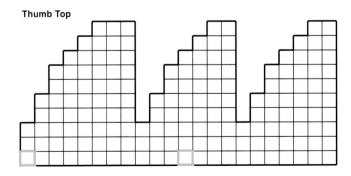

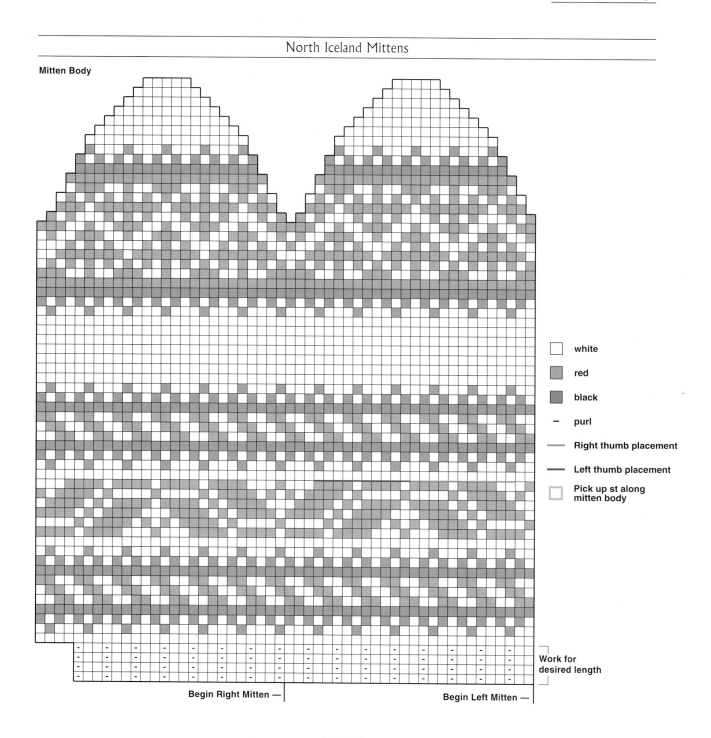

North Iceland Mittens

Mitten Body

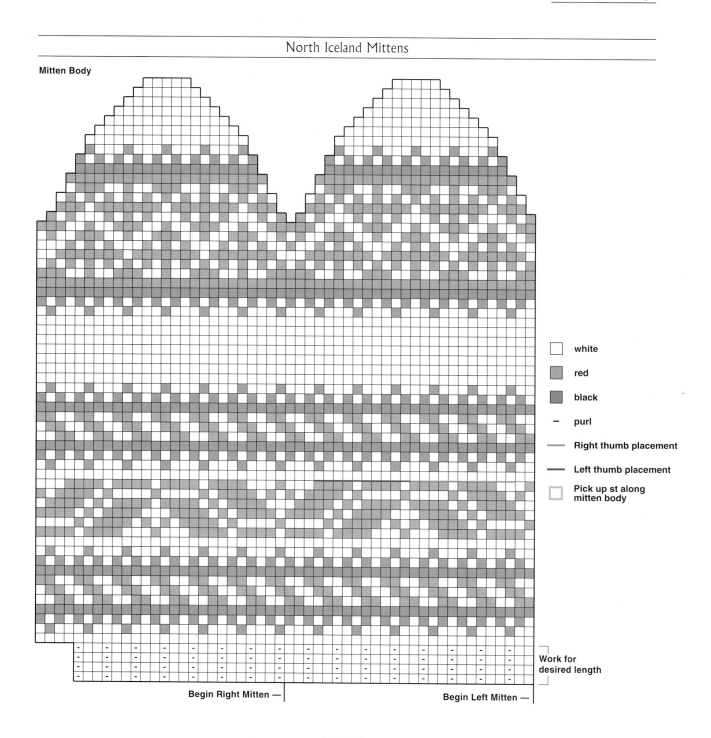

white

red

black

- purl

Right thumb placement

Left thumb placement

Pick up st along mitten body

Work for desired length

Begin Right Mitten —

Begin Left Mitten —

Lopi Mittens

Iceland's *lopi* yarn was used to knit these soft, pleasing mittens. The pattern, Jacob's ladder, was copied from a cardigan.

Finished Size: 7 1/2" (19 cm) around by 9 1/2" (24 cm) long.

Materials: 2 oz (56.5 g) white worsted-weight lopi; 2 oz (56.5 g) black worsted-weight lopi; size 5 (3.75 mm) double-pointed needles.

Gauge: 12 sts = 2" (5 cm).

Mitten body: With black and white and using 2-color CO with the black yarn over the thumb and the white yarn over the index finger (see Techniques, page 10), CO 44 sts. Join. Plait 2 rnds (see Techniques, page 11) as follows: *Rnd 1:* With both yarns forward, *p1 black, p1 white, bringing the color to be used *over*

the color not used; rep from *. *Rnd 2:* With both yarns forward, *p1 black, p1 white, bringing the color to be used *over* the color not used; rep from *. Work as charted for 26 rnds. On next rnd, with contrasting waste yarn, mark peasant thumb over 9 sts as shown. Cont as charted until piece measures to 1/2" (1.3 cm) above little finger. Work flat dec as charted. Draw up rem sts. **Thumb:** Remove waste yarn, place 18 thumb sts on needles, pick up 1 st each side, and join—20 sts. Work as charted or until piece measures to middle of thumbnail. Work flat dec as charted. Draw up rem sts. Finger-knit a small loop (see page 18) and attach it to one mitten and a button to the other.

Lopi Mittens

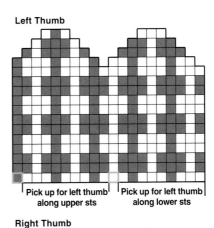

Left Thumb

| Pick up for left thumb along upper sts | Pick up for left thumb along lower sts |

Right Thumb

| Pick up for right thumb along upper sts | Pick up for right thumb along lower sts |

Lopi Mittens

Mitten Body

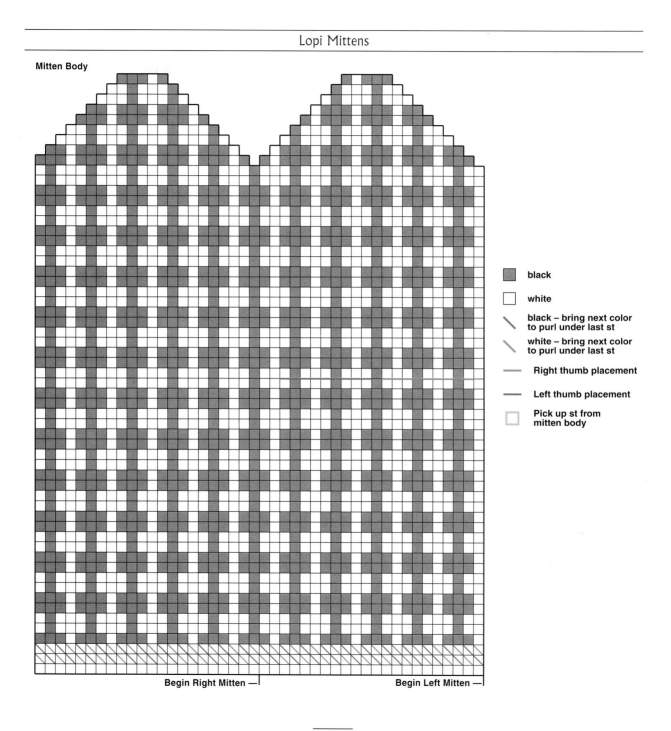

■	black
□	white
╲	black – bring next color to purl under last st
╲	white – bring next color to purl under last st
—	Right thumb placement
—	Left thumb placement
▫	Pick up st from mitten body

Begin Right Mitten —

Begin Left Mitten —

Northern European Fisherfolk

The knitting of the seaman's jersey is as old a tradition as can be found in Europe. The practical, hard-wearing, textured sweaters are knit in every fishing community along the North Sea and can't be attributed to any individual country. The jersey was first knit to replace the fishermen's inner smock and in time it became outerwear, much like the T-shirt today.

Jerseys were made with a yarn called "seaman's iron" that was spun with a very firm twist so that even the poorest fleece could be utilized. They were usually knit in dignified darker colors. The Dutch traditionally used Nassau blue, a blue yarn spun with red threads. Jerseys were so tightly worked that they could "turn water" and with age would develop a sheen. Finer, softer wool was used for wedding sweaters. As a bride-to-be knit, she would pull out strands of her hair and knit them into the sweater, adding strength and symbolically binding herself to her beloved. These sweaters were worn at the wedding, and on Sundays and holidays.

A fisherman's life, beginning at the age of seven or eight, was full of danger, hardship, and unforeseen events at sea. Their dependence on the elements made fishermen highly superstitious. Motifs knit into their jerseys took on symbolic meanings of protection and bountiful fish harvests. The patterns and pattern combinations knit into jerseys also identified home ports and parishes, family history, and the number of sons in the family. Bodies of men lost at sea that later washed up were identified by the jerseys they wore so they could be returned home for burial. Before a man was buried at sea, his jersey was removed and returned to his wife, who could choose to keep the jersey or bury it in her family cemetery.

Girls were taught to knit when they were young. To spur them on, their mothers would conceal a few pennies inside the balls of yarn. When a girl used all the yarn in a ball, she was allowed to buy candy with the pennies.

When women traveled by boat and the weather turned foggy, the distance traveled could be figured by the length of knitting that had been produced.

During lean times, knitting augmented incomes. As knitting became more profitable, other work was at times left undone. In the early seventeenth century on the Channel Islands, a law was enacted to prohibit knitting during the fall harvest or vraic-cutting season under penalty of imprisonment in the castle on bread and water. (Vraic is a seaweed used as fuel or fertilizer.) The Island of Jersey passed a law in the same era compelling all people over the age of fifteen to relinquish knitting and assist farmers with the vraic and corn harvests.

The artistry in the seaman's jerseys pays tribute to the creative character of the craftswomen who knit them. "Fish-wives" had responsibilities that stretched from sunup to sundown. Knitting gave them the opportunity to rest and creatively express themselves without the stigma of idleness.

Fisherman's Mittens

These mittens incorporate two of the numerous jersey textured patterns used by communities that lined Europe's Atlantic coast.

Flags were an important means of communication before the radio was invented. The color and location of flags on the ship heralded the size of a catch or signalled that a crew member was ill or had died.

The ladder represents the steps up the cliff from the harbor to the village and the safety of home. It was also referred to as Jacob's ladder, symbolizing man's climb to heaven.

Fisherman's Mittens

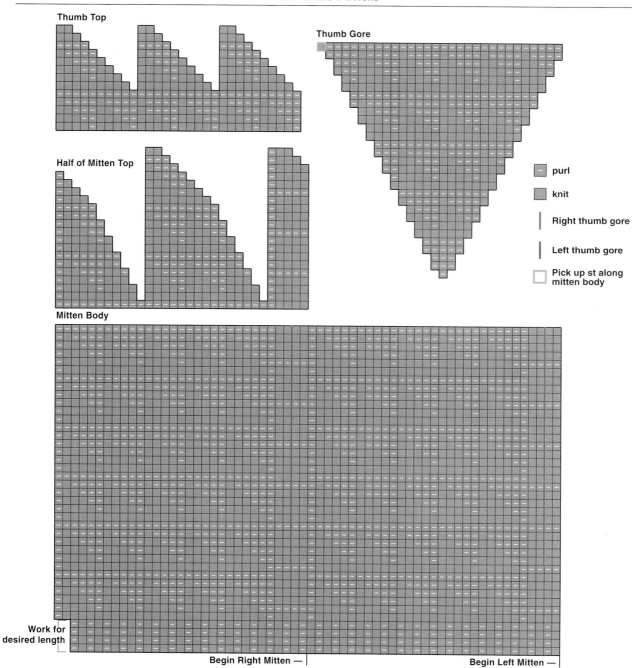

Thumb Top

Thumb Gore

Half of Mitten Top

Mitten Body

Work for desired length

purl

knit

| Right thumb gore

| Left thumb gore

☐ Pick up st along mitten body

Begin Right Mitten —|

Begin Left Mitten —|

Finished Size: 7 ¾" (19.5 cm) around by 7" (18 cm) long, excluding cuff.

Materials: 4 oz (113.5 g) navy worsted-weight wool; size 1 (2.25 mm) double-pointed needles.

Gauge: 16 sts = 2" (5 cm).

Mitten body: CO 60 sts. Join. Work 1x1 rib for desired length, then inc 2 sts evenly spaced—62 sts. Work as charted for 6 more rnds. On next rnd, begin normal thumb gore and work as charted for 29 rnds—29 thumb sts. Place thumb sts on yarn length. Cont across rnd, CO 1 st over held thumb sts, and rejoin—62 sts. Cont even until piece measures to tip of little finger. Work 4-point dec as charted. Draw up rem sts. **Thumb:** Place thumb sts on needles, pick up 1 st along the mitten body, and join—30 sts. Work even until piece measures to middle of thumbnail. Work 3-point dec as charted. Draw up rem sts.

The Faeroe Islands

The Faeroe Islands, which means "Sheep" Islands, are between Iceland and Scotland in the north Atlantic. Few trees or bushes grow in the volcanic soils, and ocean winds sweep unchecked over the eighteen islands. Only the Gulf Stream helps moderate the long, wet winters.

Wool, called "Faeroe Gold", was closely interwoven with the culture. Nearly everyone owned sheep, which were free to roam the village. In preparation for winter, everyone from schoolchildren to sea captains helped gather hay to feed the sheep during the months when pasture would be scarce. Islanders used wool to barter for everything from household goods to timber for building houses and boats. Wool paid rent, taxes, and court fines.

The quality of wool produced by the sheep of the Faeroe Islands depended on the prior winter's weather. High rainfall and strong winds would produce long hairy fibers, yielding a strong yarn. A mild winter with plentiful grass favored the softer undercoat and a finer wool. The wool was "skubbered" or plucked from the sheep in the early summer when the growth of new wool loosened the old coat. Because there were no sharp ends from shearing, the yarn produced was gentle to the skin.

Knitting occupied every spare minute of the islander's time. Men were responsible for carding and spinning the wool while women did the knitting. Children went wool-gathering to collect tufts caught on bushes; no wool could go to waste. Children were required to knit an allotted number of rows before they went out to play.

Much of the knitting was done for seafaring men. For an expedition to Iceland, a two-month voyage, four changes of clothes were needed. A trip to Greenland, a voyage lasting four months, required at least seven changes of clothes. It was a matter of household pride, as well as one of survival, to send a large amount of knitted clothing with the seafaring man.

Folklore dictated that no knitting was done for men between Christmas and New Year's Day because the islanders believed that if a sweater made during that time was worn to sea, the wearer would not return. Garments made during this time could be sold, however.

Most yarns were spun to a sport-weight size. Garments were knit loose and rather large, then felted to size for added protection against wind and rain. Geometric shapes worked in dark colors on a light background were traditional.

Faeroe Island Mittens

This pattern was originally knit into men's formal vests, usually felted and brushed and worn on Sundays and for special celebrations.

Finished Size: 7 1/2" (19 cm) around by 7 3/4" (19.5 cm) long, excluding cuff.
Materials: 1 1/2 oz (42.5 g) navy sport-weight wool; 1 oz (28.5 g) light blue sport-weight wool; size 2 (2.75 mm) double-pointed needles.
Gauge: 19 sts = 2" (5 cm).

Mitten body: With navy, CO 60 sts. Join. Work 2x1 rib for desired length, then change to body pattern and inc 10 sts—70 sts. Work as charted for 1 more rnd. On next rnd, begin normal thumb gore and work as charted for 26 rnds—27 thumb sts. Place thumb sts on yarn length. Cont across rnd, CO 1 st over held thumb sts, and rejoin—70 sts. Work as charted until piece measures to tip of little finger. Work flat dec as charted. Draw

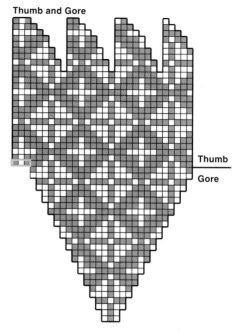

Faeroe Island Mittens

Thumb and Gore

Thumb

Gore

Faeroe Island Mittens

Mitten Body

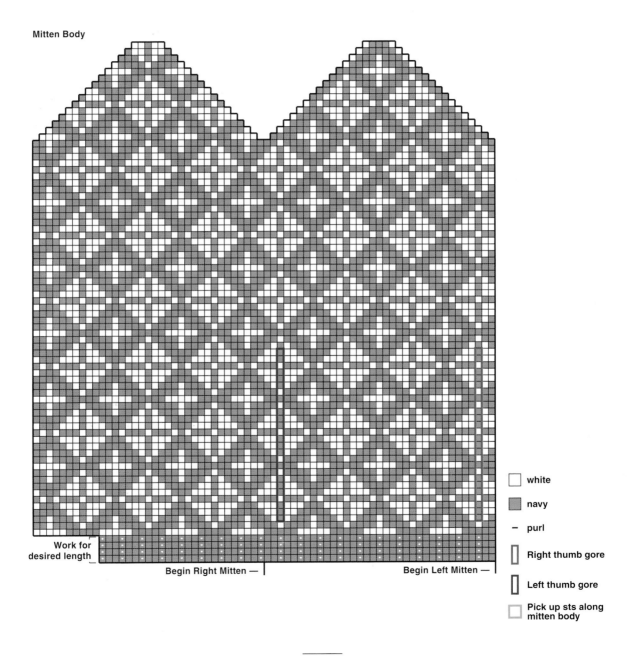

Work for desired length

Begin Right Mitten —

Begin Left Mitten —

□ white

■ navy

- purl

▯ Right thumb gore

▮ Left thumb gore

□ Pick up sts along mitten body

up rem sts. **Thumb:** Place thumb sts on needles, pick up 3 sts along the mitten body, and join—30 sts. Work as charted or until piece measures to middle of thumbnail. Work 4-point dec as charted. Draw up rem sts.

This mitten is sized large so that it can be lightly felted to size.

Greece

Greece is a mountainous country located on the southern portion of the Balkan peninsula. Its peaks are snow-covered year round, including the mythical home of Zeus, Mount Olympus.

Historically, the majority of Greeks earned their livelihoods as farmers. Women and men shared the task of caring for the olive orchards and vineyards that covered the mountainsides. Men were responsible for shepherding flocks of goats and sheep on the higher slopes where the rocky soils were not suitable for cultivation. Women were responsible for spinning, knitting, and weaving in addition to daily household chores.

Knitters made stockings and leggings as well as sweaters, arm bands, caps, and gloves with bright contrasting colors in sharp geometric designs. Garments for special occasions were tightly knit in worsted-weight wool, yielding a firm, inflexible fabric, and were brightly decorated. Greek knitters used the Eastern method of knitting, beginning at the tip and ending at the cuff.

The Greek Mitten

Tightly knit arm bands that Greek men wore on their forearms below blousey sleeves provided the inspiration for this mitten.

Finished Size: 8" (20.5 cm) around by 9" (23 cm) long.
Materials: 3 oz (85 g) black worsted-weight wool; 3 oz (85 g) white worsted-weight wool; size 0 (2 mm) double-pointed needles.
Gauge: 22 sts = 2" (5 cm).

Thumb: With black and using the Eastern knitting method (see Techniques, page 16), CO 5 sts. Work flat incs as charted—38 sts. Cont to end of thumb as charted. Place sts on two holders (19 sts on each). **Mitten body:** With black and using the Eastern knitting method, CO 22 sts. Join. Work 2 rnds as charted. On the next rnd, begin flat incs and work as charted until there are 86 sts. Cont as chart-

The Greek Mitten

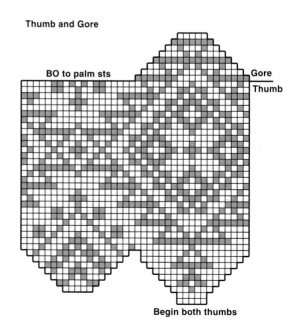

Thumb and Gore

BO to palm sts

Gore

Thumb

Begin both thumbs

The Greek Mitten

*These mittens, with a typical strong geometric design, were knit with
the Eastern method, beginning at the tips and ending at the cuffs.*

The Greek Mitten

Mitten Body

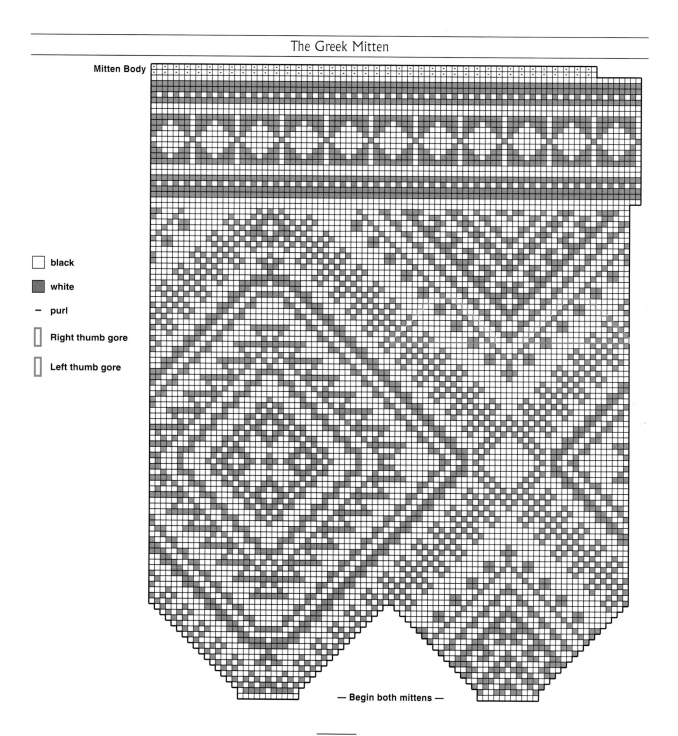

black

white

– purl

Right thumb gore

Left thumb gore

— Begin both mittens —

ed, attaching thumb by binding off 19 inner thumb sts together with 19 palm sts where shown. On the next rnd, work rem 19 outer thumb sts over the 19 BO sts—86 sts. Note that the gore pattern extends into the body, interrupting the body pattern. At cuff, inc 2 sts evenly spaced—88 sts. Work cuff as charted. Then dec 8 sts evenly spaced—80 sts. Work 1x1 rib for 2 rnds. BO all sts loosely.

Bosnia

Bosnia is on the Balkan peninsula in the eastern Alps. This mountainous country, covered with forest and farmland, has been referred to as "Little Switzerland", and its high elevations are known for their long, severe winters. It is home to many cultures and ethnic groups. Most Bosnians live in the country, working as farmers and shepherds, and the region is known for its hard-working sheep dogs. According to folk legend, one dog can easily care for up to 2,000 animals and fight off several wolves at once.

Women spin and knit and are responsible for providing warm clothing for their families. In times of hardship, women sell knitted goods to help provide for their families.

The Bosnian Mitten

The motif on this mitten comes from a Bosnian slipper sock.

Finished Size: 8 ½" (21.5 cm) around by 9 ½" (24 cm) long.
Materials: 2 oz (56.5 g) black sport-weight wool; 1 ½ oz (42.5 g) white sport-weight wool; size 1 (2.25 mm) double-pointed needles.
Gauge: 20 sts = 2" (5 cm).

The Bosnian Mitten

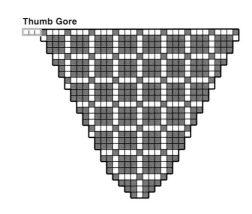

Thumb Gore

Thumb Top

The Bosnian Mitten

Mitten Body

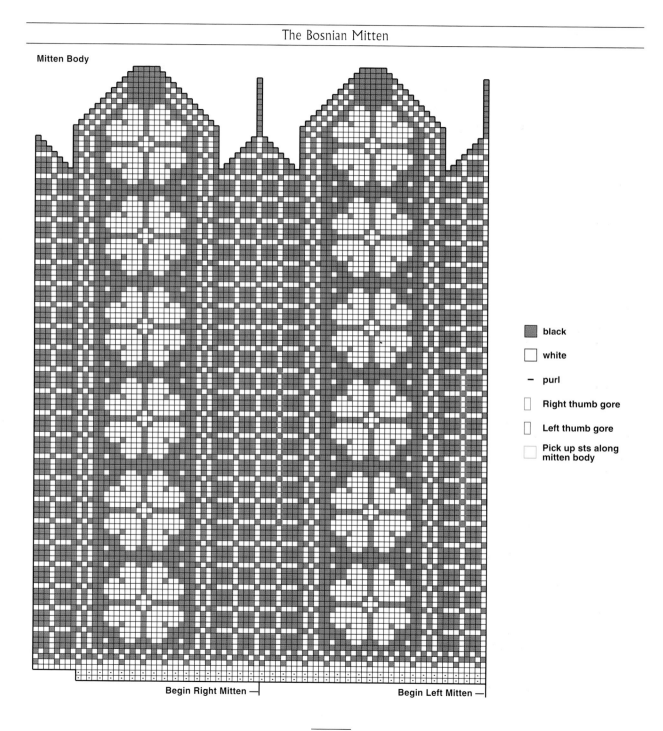

black

white

— purl

Right thumb gore

Left thumb gore

Pick up sts along mitten body

Begin Right Mitten —|

Begin Left Mitten —|

Mitten body: With white, CO 76 sts. Join. Work 1x1 rib for 2 rnds, then change to body pattern and inc 8 sts evenly spaced—84 sts. Work as charted for 26 more rnds. On next rnd, work normal thumb gore as charted for 28 rnds—33 thumb sts. Place thumb sts on yarn length. Cont across rnd, CO 1 st over held thumb sts, and rejoin—84 sts. Cont as charted, working flat dec as shown. Draw up rem sts. **Thumb:** Place thumb sts on needle, pick up 3 sts over CO st along the mitten body, and join—36 sts. Cont in pattern until piece measures to middle of thumbnail. Work 3-point dec as charted. Draw up rem sts.

Finished Size: 8 ½" (21.5 cm) around by 7 ½" (19 cm) long, excluding cuff.

Materials: 2 oz (56.5 g) black worsted-weight wool; ½ oz (14 g) each of six contrasting colors of worsted-weight wool; size 2 (2.75 mm) double-pointed needles.

Gauge: 17 sts = 2" (5 cm).

Thumb: With black and using the Eastern knitting method (see Techniques, page 16), CO 10 sts.

Albania

On the Balkan peninsula along the shores of the Adriatic Sea, Albania's terrain ranges from rolling hills to the snow-covered peaks of the Albanian Alps. More than half of Albania lies at least 2,000 feet (610 m) above sea level.

Most Albanian men were farmers and shepherds of goats and sheep. Women helped with farm chores, kept house, and clothed the family. Before an Albanian wedding, the groom's family presented the bride with a hope chest filled with knit and woven clothing, jewelry, and coffee, as well as sugar, representing the sweetness of the honeymoon.

Brightly dyed red, yellow, and green wool was knit on black in horizontal bands of geometric designs for stockings and mitten cuffs. Albanian knitters use the Eastern knitting technique of beginning at the top and working toward the cuff.

Albanian Mittens

The pattern in this mitten comes from traditional Albanian stockings.

Albanian Mittens

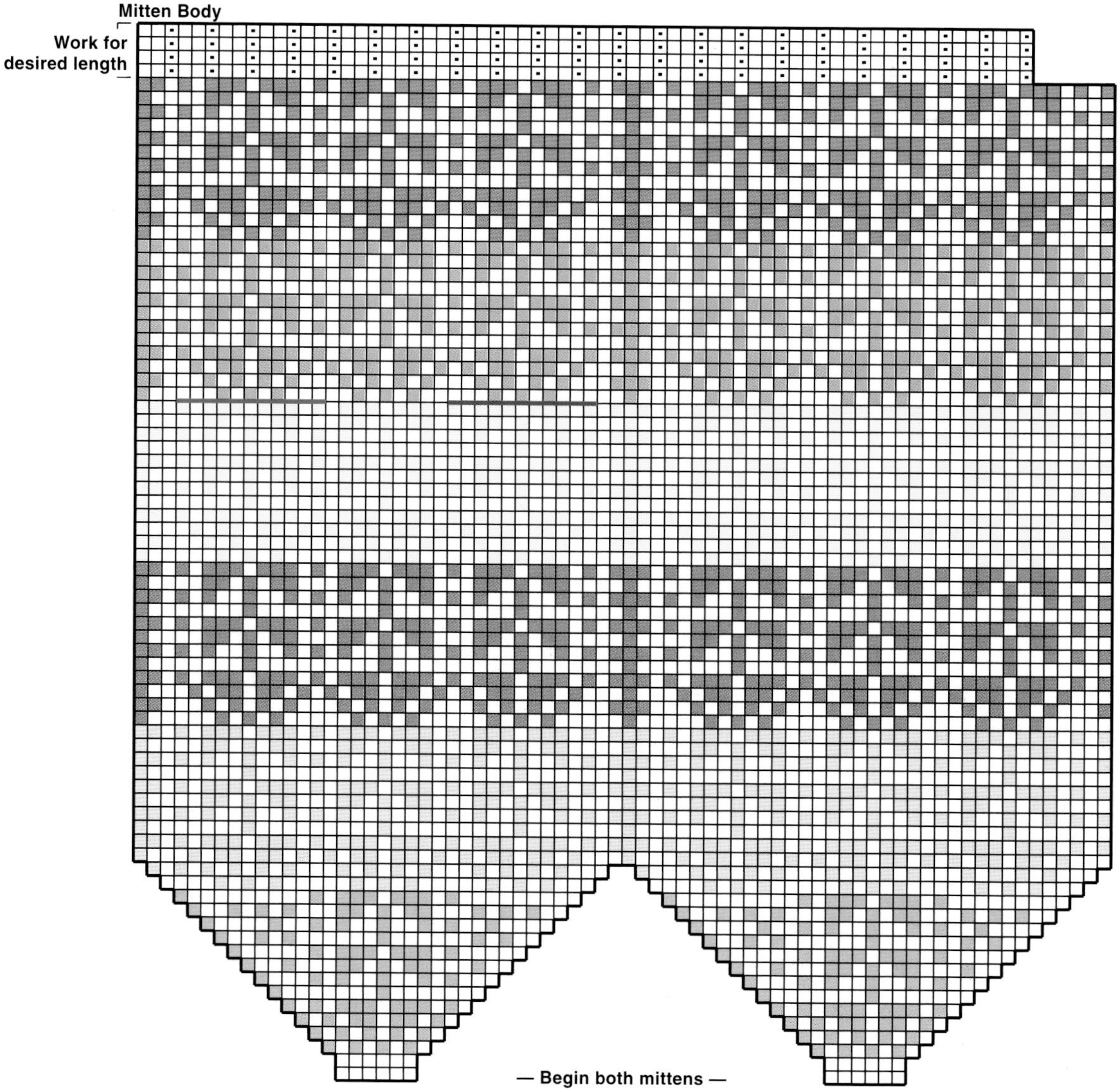

Mitten Body

Work for desired length

— Begin both mittens —

	black		yellow		pink		red		Right thumb placement
	magenta		green		navy	–	purl		Left thumb placement

Albanian Mittens

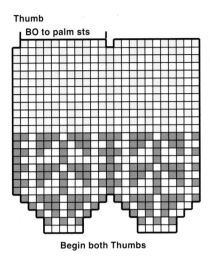

Thumb
BO to palm sts

Begin both Thumbs

Work 2 rnds then work flat incs as charted—24 sts. Cont as charted, dec 1 st at each side in last row— 22 sts. Place sts on two stitch holders (11 sts each holder). ***Mitten body:*** With black and using the Eastern knitting method, CO 12 sts. Join. Work chart for 2 rnds. On the next rnd, begin flat incs and work as charted until there are 72 sts. Cont to thumb insertion. Attach thumb by binding off 11 inner thumb sts tog with 11 palm sts. On next rnd, work rem 11 thumb sts over the 11 BO sts —72 sts. Work to end of color patterning, then dec 6 sts evenly spaced— 66 sts. Work 2x1 rib for desired length. BO all sts loosely.

England

In the first century A.D., wool brought wealth and power to England. For the next 1,700 years, the fate of wool was England's fate. Parliament has placed a woolsack on the chair of the Lord Chancellor, speaker of the House of Lords, since the 1300s to remind the lords of wool's importance. Shepherds were buried with a tuft of wool upon their chests to explain to their Creator why they never attended church on Sundays.

Knitting involved all of England. Families gathered for "sittings" in the evenings. By the light of a peat fire they would talk, sing, and knit, telling riddles or listening as someone read from the Bible, *Robinson Crusoe,* or *Pilgrims Progress.* Sittings were an opportunity for young people to meet for courtship, and they were enlivened with knitting races—knitters were given equal lengths of yarn and strove to finish first. Special knitting songs were sung, the faster the rhythm the quicker the fingers. Yarn was wound around a hollow rattle containing pebbles so that as the night grew old and the light dimmed, an escaped ball of yarn could be found.

Many peasants depended on knitting for their livelihoods; though labor-intensive, it used readily available natural resources. Esther Benzeille in *Cottage Comforts,* 1825, describes the importance of knitting to the common folk.

It is work that may be taken up and laid down in a moment. A set of needles may be bought for a penny and a ball of worsted for another. It may be done at any light or with a child in the arms; and when you are tired of stirring work, knitting serves well for a rest. In the summer you can take a walk in your garden and knit as you go. . . . A good knitter, too, has generally got employment, if she chooses to take it in; and if the scraps of time so employed add but a sixpence to her weekly income, it is not to be despised. She may sit and blow the fire long enough before she finds a sixpence in the ashes, or loll over her thatch long enough before she sees one roll down the street.

In 1589, William Lee of Nottingham made the first knitting machine. History records that he resolved to build it when he felt ignored by his sweetheart, who spent all her free time knitting socks. Queen Elizabeth I refused to grant a patent for its widespread construction, saying "I have too much love for my people who obtain their bread by the employment of knitting, to . . . forward an invention that will tend to their ruin." She was successful in postponing its use for many years.

Northern England's Dales were famous for their finely knit gloves, which were noted for providing a firm grip on horse reins no matter how wet. The gloves were knit in contrasting light and dark yarns: black, dark gray, navy, or brown with pale blue, white, yellow, or cream. Boxed or plaid motifs covered the palms, while fingers and thumbs featured a pattern called "salt and pepper". Cuffs knit with red linings typically included names and dates. Young children helped by knitting the cuffs and skillful elders finished the gloves. They were knit with side seam thumb gussets and could be worn on either hand.

The English Dales Mitten

Gloves knit in the English Dales inspired this mitten. The thumb has salt-and-pepper patterning and the body is shepherd's plaid. A cuff lining, added for warmth, is red.

The English Dales Mitten

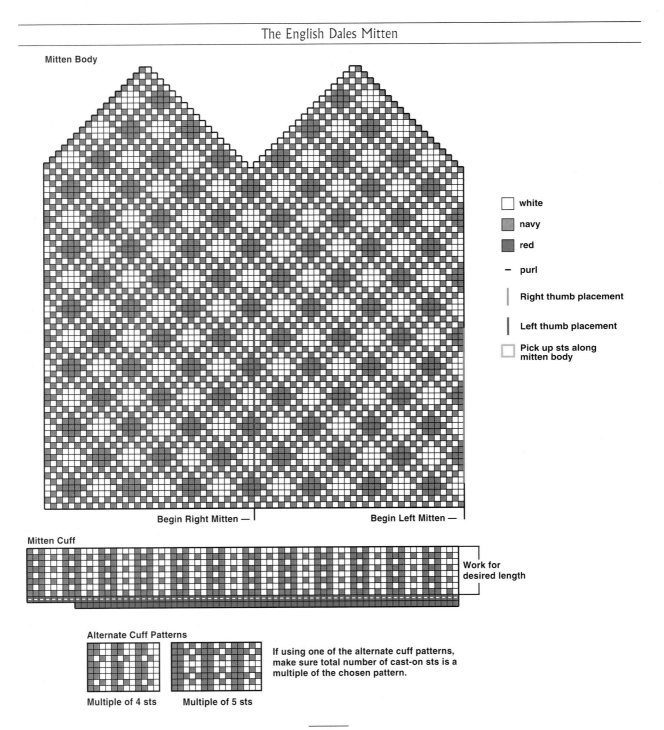

Mitten Body

white
navy
red
– purl
| Right thumb placement
| Left thumb placement
☐ Pick up sts along mitten body

Begin Right Mitten — Begin Left Mitten —

Mitten Cuff

Work for desired length

Alternate Cuff Patterns

Multiple of 4 sts   Multiple of 5 sts

If using one of the alternate cuff patterns, make sure total number of cast-on sts is a multiple of the chosen pattern.

The English Dales Mitten

Thumb Top

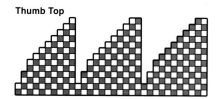

Thumb Gore

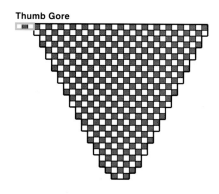

Finished Size: 8 ¼" (21 cm) around by 8" (20.5 cm) long, excluding cuff.

Materials: 1 ½ oz (42.5 g) navy sport-weight wool; 1 ½ oz (42.5 g) white sport-weight wool; ½ oz (14 g) red sport-weight wool; size 2 (2.75 mm) double-pointed needles.

Gauge: 17 sts = 2" (5 cm).

Mitten body: With red, CO 64 sts. Join. Work St st lining to desired cuff length. Purl 1 rnd, inc 8 sts evenly spaced—72 sts. Work charted cuff to match lining length, then dec 2 sts evenly spaced—70 sts. Work body pattern as charted for 4 rnds. On next rnd, begin side seam thumb gore and work as charted for 26 rnds—29 thumb sts. Place thumb sts on

yarn length. Cont across rnd and rejoin—70 sts. Work as charted or until piece measures to tip of little finger. Work flat dec as charted. Draw up rem sts. ***Thumb:*** Place thumb sts on needle, pick up 3 sts along the mitten body, and join—32 sts. Work until piece measures to middle of thumbnail. Work 3-point dec as charted. Draw up rem sts.

Fair Isle

Fair Isle is one of the Shetland Islands, located where the North Sea becomes the Atlantic Ocean. Known for their wild weather and foggy seas, the islands are home to a people who were first fishermen, then farmers, leading difficult lives in harsh circumstances.

Shetland knitting dates to the sixteenth century. Then and for the next two centuries, knitting had great economic importance. Fishing paid the rent and farming provided oatmeal, potatoes, and milk, but knitted goods bartered with merchant shippers paid for everything else.

The sheep of Shetland were small and sturdy, perfectly suited to thrive on the island's harsh climate and moorland pasture. Their wool is renowned for its soft, silky firmness.

Early Shetland knitting was worked in one color. Knitters first used multiple colors in detailed patterns on Fair Isle and the origin of the style has been the subject of much speculation. One legend has it that in 1588 a shipwrecked sailor from the Spanish Armada taught the technique to the islanders. Another tale recounts that local women adapted the pattern from a woven shawl brought back from the Baltics by one of their seafaring men.

Fair Isle knitting has evolved into a panorama of colors and shades worked into a multitude of patterns. The intricate color play is even worked into the ribbings of some garments.

Basic Rules of Fair Isle Knitting:

(1) Only two colors are used per round; one for the patterning and the other for the background. Colors are changed frequently with no more than seven consecutive stitches of one color.

(2) The patterning consists primarily of diagonal lines; vertical lines are kept to a minimum. Diagonal lines distribute the point of tension created between color changes from one round to the next.

(3) Patterns are symmetrical and are worked over an odd number of rounds.

In the earliest Fair Isle knitting, diagonal OXO patterning was most common. The X is thought to represent the cross of St. Andrew.

Fair Isle Mittens

Finished Size: 8 ½" (21.5 cm) around by 7 ¾" (19.5 cm) long, excluding cuff.

Materials: 2 oz (56.5 g) background color sport-weight wool; ½ oz (14 g) each of several secondary

---

Fair Isle Mittens

Right Thumb

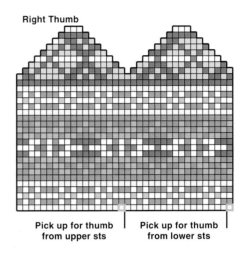

Pick up for thumb from upper sts | **Pick up for thumb from lower sts**

Left Thumb

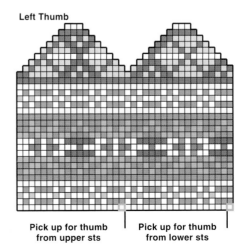

Pick up for thumb from upper sts | **Pick up for thumb from lower sts**

Fair Isle Mittens

Mitten Body

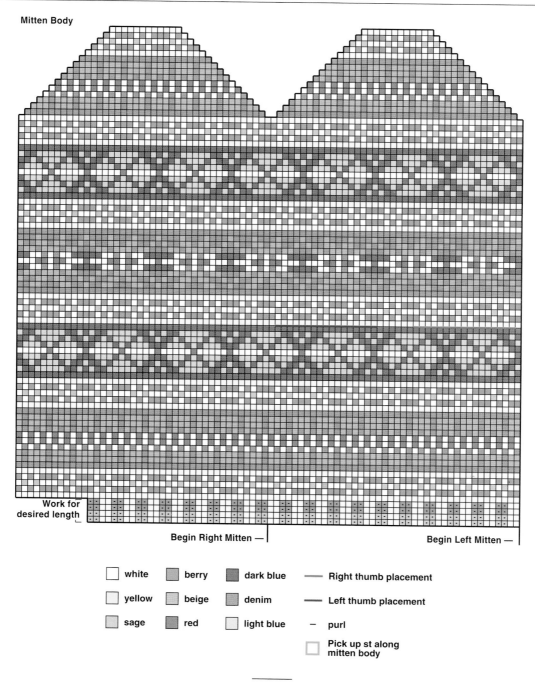

Work for desired length

Begin Right Mitten —   Begin Left Mitten —

	white		berry		dark blue	——	Right thumb placement
	yellow		beige		denim	——	Left thumb placement
	sage		red		light blue	–	purl
						☐	Pick up st along mitten body

color sport-weight wool; contrasting waste yarn; size 1 (2.25 mm) double-pointed needles.
Gauge: 20 sts = 2" (5 cm).

Mitten body: With background color, CO 72 sts. Join. Work 2x2 corrugated rib for desired length, then change to body pattern and inc 12 sts evenly spaced—84 sts. Work as charted for 28 more rnds. On next rnd, with contrasting waste yarn, mark peasant thumb over 17 sts as shown. Cont as charted or until piece measures to tip of little finger. Work flat dec as charted. Graft rem 24 sts with Kitchener st. **Thumb:** Remove waste yarn, place 34 thumb sts on needles, pick up 1 st each side, and join—36 sts. Work as charted or until piece measures to middle of thumbnail. Work flat dec as charted. Graft rem 6 sts with Kitchener st.

The Aran Islands

Off the west coast of Ireland in the mouth of Galway Bay lie the islands of Aran. For centuries the inhabitants of these rocky isles have braved the Atlantic's inhospitable climate while they fished. Like other fishermen along the northern European coastline, they wore heavily textured knit tops called jerseys.

What made Aran's jerseys unique were the use of creamy white 5-ply wool, called *baínin*, that was spun and knit "in the grease" (i.e., it contained a lot of lanolin) to increase its water-repellency, and the generous use of textured patterns. Other cultures considered undyed wool poor and shameful, but few can deny the beauty of these garments rich in intricate, vertical panels of braiding, twisting, and interlocking patterns. These patterns were practical, for they maximized the thermal insulation properties of wool and trapped air while retaining the natural elasticity of the knitted fabric.

The patterns found on these jerseys is reminescent of the Celtic art of "knotwork". Celtic knotwork was a mathematically-based interlacing art worked into stone, metal, and manuscripts. These interlacing patterns knitted into jerseys have, over time, been given names drawn from the islanders' lives, works, and relationships with God. Stitches based on the imagery of life at sea are most numerous. The familiar coil-o-rope, or cable pattern, depicted the ropes used to rig and sail the ships. Bobbles represented men in a *curragh*, the traditional canvas-covered fishing craft, while other motifs represent nets, anchors, lobster claws, and creels. Familiar stitches include the moss stitch (named for the moss that covers most everything exposed to the damp island environment), the tree of life (symbolizing long

Aran Island Mittens

Mitten Body

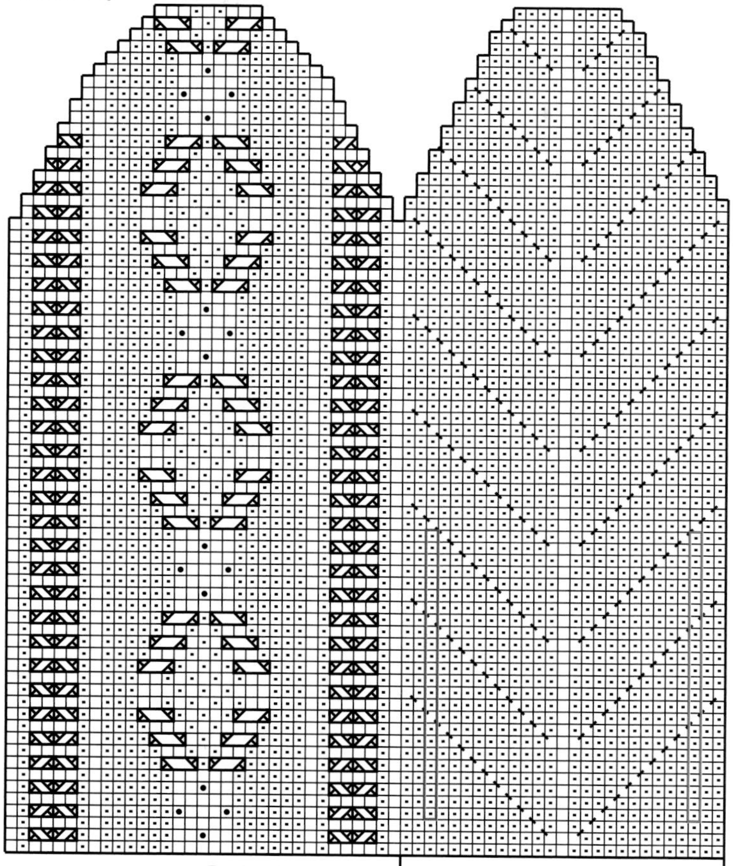

Begin Right Mitten —

Begin Left Mitten —

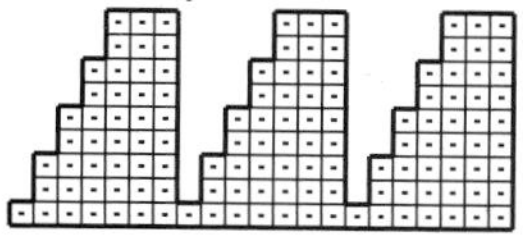

Mitten Cuff

Begin both mittens —

☐ knit

– purl

∕ knit second st, then purl first st

∖ purl second st tbl, then knit first st

● bobble – knit into back, front, then back of st, making 3 sts, turn, p3, turn, k3, turn, p3, turn, sl 1, k2tog, psso

◩ 2/2 RC – place 2 sts on cn to back, k2, k2 on cn

◩ 2/1 RCP – place 1 st on cn to back, k2, p1 on cn

◪ 2/1 LCP – place 2 sts on cn to front, p1, k2 on cn

◩ 1/1 RC – place 1 st on cn to back, k1, k1 on cn

◪ 1/1 LC – place 1 st on cn to front, k1, k1 on cn

☐ Right thumb gore

☐ Left thumb gore

☐ Pick up sts along mitten body

Thumb Top

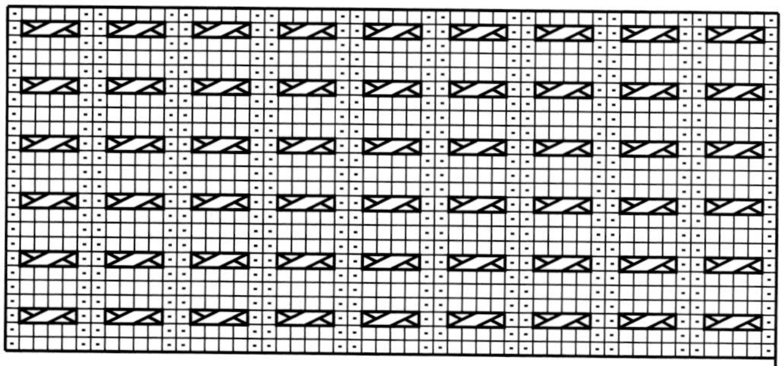

Thumb Gore

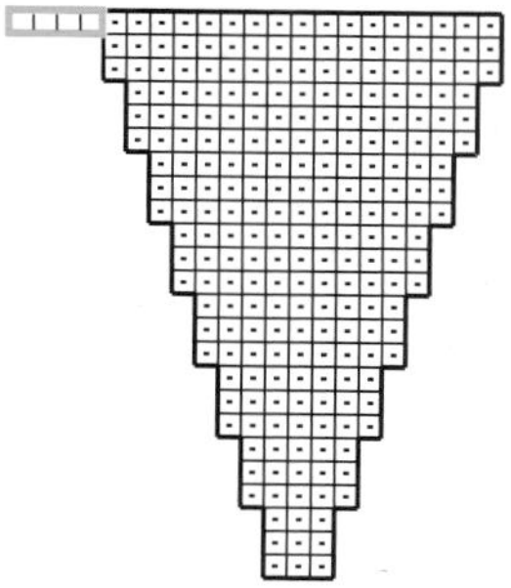

life and many sons to carry on the fisherman's work), and the honeycomb (symbolic of hard work—the industrious bee bringing its just reward, honey). The honeycomb stitch, knit singular and vertically, also represents the link between God and man.

Aran Island Mittens

These mittens draw their patterning from the traditional jerseys of the Aran fishermen.

Finished Size: 8" (20.5 cm) around by 10" (25.5 cm) long, including cuff.
Materials: 4 oz (113.5 g) natural cream worsted-weight wool; size 3 (3.25 mm) double-pointed needles.
Gauge: 12 sts = 2" (5 cm) in rev St st.

Mitten body: CO 54 sts. Join. Work 4x2 cabled rib as charted or for desired length, then change to body pattern and inc 6 sts evenly spaced—60 sts. Work as charted for 2 more rnds. On next rnd, begin normal thumb gore. Work gore sts in rev St st as charted for 24 rnds—17 thumb sts. Place thumb sts on yarn length. Rejoin and cont as charted until piece measures to tip of little finger. Work flat dec as charted. Graft rem 18 sts with Kitchener st. *Thumb:* Place thumb sts on needles, pick up 4 sts along the mitten body, and join—21 sts. Work in rev St st until mitten thumb measures to middle of thumbnail. Work 3-point dec as charted. Draw up rem sts.

Austria and Bavaria

The Alpine region of central Europe is home to richly textured knitting renowned for its traveling, interlacing knit stitches, cables, and knots worked on a purl background. This knitting style is distinguished from other textured knitting traditions by the twisted knit stitch that gives a raised effect to the pattern. This heavy fabric, worked in the natural cream of sheep's wool, reflects the rural robustness of densely forested terrain.

Knitters of old, living in villages in the woods, were isolated from other communities except by tedious, time-consuming travel on foot or by animal. These patterns remind us of the switchback trails and rock-strewn paths the inhabitants journeyed along and the gnarled old trees which still grow in the alpine woodland today. This knitting tradition dates to the eighteenth century, when it was first used in stockings worn by men.

Schools are keeping the region's rich knitting heritage alive. A second-grader's first knitting project is typically a pair of mittens. To entice young knitters, teachers hide small presents inside their balls of yarn to be revealed as the knitting progresses.

Austrian Tyrolean knitting can differ from Bavarian knitting by the addition of embroidered flowers that celebrate the floral splendor of the local mountainsides in late spring.

Tyrolean Mittens

The neighboring Alpine regions of Austria and Bavaria first used these richly textured patterns in men's stockings. Austria's Tyrolean knitters liberally sprinkled their work with brightly embroidered flowers.

Finished Size: 8 1/2" (21.5 cm) around by 7 1/2" (19 cm) long, excluding cuff.
Materials: 4 oz (113.5 g) cream worsted-weight wool; size 3 (3.25 mm) double-pointed needles.

Gauge: 14 sts = 2" (5 cm) (palm section); 18 sts = 2" (5 cm), (back section).

Mitten body: CO 60 sts. Join. Work 1x1 twisted rib as charted for desired length, then change to body pattern and inc 12 sts evenly spaced—72 sts. Work as charted for 3 more rnds. On next rnd, begin normal thumb gore and work as charted for 23 rnds— 24 thumb sts. Place thumb sts on yarn length. Cont across rnd, CO 1 st over held thumb sts, and rejoin— 72 sts. Cont as charted or until piece measures to tip of little finger. Work flat dec as charted. Graft rem 24 sts with kitchener st. **Thumb:** Place thumb sts on needle, pick up 4 sts along CO st along the mitten body, and join—28 sts. Work as charted or until piece measures to middle of thumbnail. Work flat dec as charted. Draw up rem sts.

Tyrolean Mittens

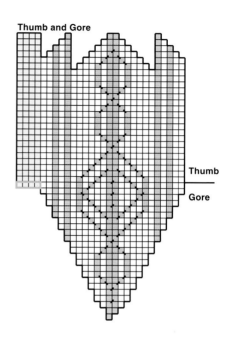

Thumb and Gore

Thumb

Gore

Embroidery: To make a mitten uniquely your own, choose brightly colored yarn and liberally embroider, using the lazy-daisy st and French knots, flowers and leaves over the back and thumb of the mitten.

Tyrolean Mittens

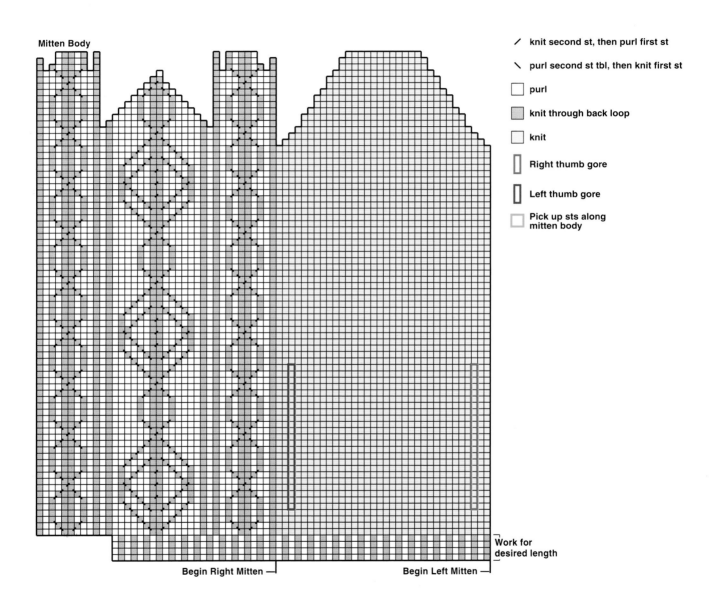

Mitten Body

knit second st, then purl first st

purl second st tbl, then knit first st

purl

knit through back loop

knit

Right thumb gore

Left thumb gore

Pick up sts along mitten body

Work for desired length

Begin Right Mitten

Begin Left Mitten

Mittens from Asia

Turkey

Turkey is a land of rugged beauty with towering mountains encircling a high semi-arid plateau. Its high altitudes are known for their bitterly cold winters.

Anatolian knitting dates to the seventeenth century and is best known for its richly patterned stockings. Turkish carpets and embroidery influenced the designs, which often revealed a wearer's community and social rank. Some symbolic patterns hid coded requests or helped ward off the evil eye. Stockings were knit to commemorate national and community events, natural disasters, or great legends. Knitted stockings were begun at the toe and worked upward to the cuff, because it was considered good luck to knit "toward the heart".

Turkish women were responsible for supplying all the knitted garments needed by their families. As knitting was more portable than Turkey's famed weaving, it often accompanied women when they were away from home. They carried the working yarn around the napes of their necks, allowing them to knit while walking or on horseback.

Traditional Anatolian knitting, worked in shades of red, blue, and gold on cream, is as colorful as the region's famous carpets and embroidery.

Anatolian Mittens

These mittens use the brightly stitched Anatolian patterns found in traditional men's stockings. Although these mittens were knit from the cuff upward, knitting from this area was done in the Eastern method.

Finished Size: 8 ¼" (21 cm) around by 10" (25.5 cm) long, including cuff.

Materials: 2 oz (56.5 g) white worsted-weight wool; 2 oz (56.5 g) red worsted-weight wool; contrasting waste yarn; size 3 (3.25 mm) double-pointed needles.

Gauge: 15 sts = 2" (5 cm).

Mitten body: With white, CO 56 sts. Join. Work 1x1 rib for 2 rnds, then inc 4 sts evenly spaced—60 sts. Work 18 rnds for cuff as charted, then inc 2 sts evenly spaced—62 sts. Work as charted for 21 more rnds. On next rnd, with contrasting waste yarn, mark peasant thumb over 13 sts as shown. Cont as charted or until piece measures to tip of little finger. Work flat dec as charted. Graft rem 10 sts with Kitchener

Anatolian Mittens

Mitten Body

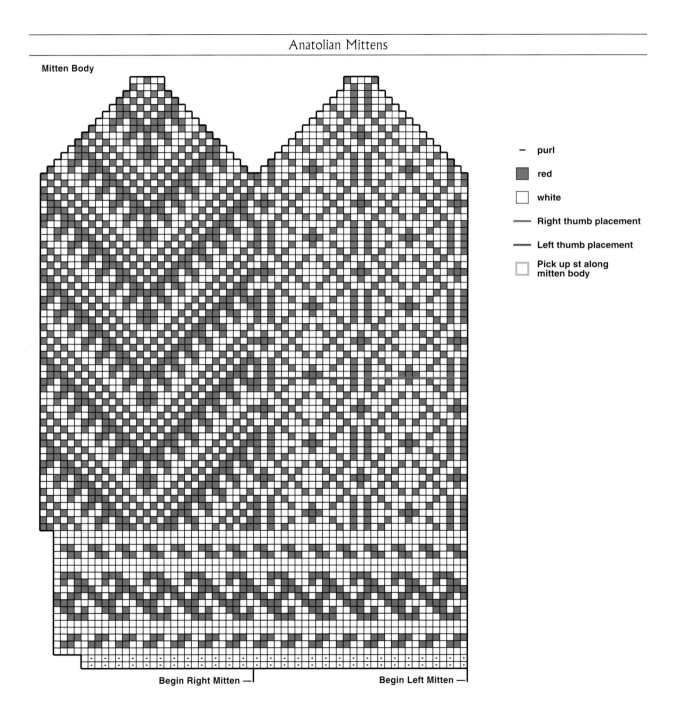

-   purl

■ red

□ white

— Right thumb placement

— Left thumb placement

▢ **Pick up st along mitten body**

Begin Right Mitten —

Begin Left Mitten —

Anatolian Mittens

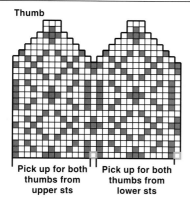

Thumb

Pick up for both thumbs from upper sts | Pick up for both thumbs from lower sts

st. **Thumb:** Remove waste yarn, place 26 thumb sts on needles, pick up 1 st each side, and join—28 sts. Work as charted or until piece measures to middle of thumbnail. Work flat dec as charted. Graft rem 6 sts with Kitchener st.

Kashmir

Located in the Himalayan mountains, Kashmir is split between India and Pakistan. One of the world's highest inhabited lands, it is appropriately called "the roof of the world". Its frozen peaks and snow-covered passes scattered with shattered rocks endure extreme sub-zero temperatures during the winter months.

These Himalayan heights are home to the renowned and agile Kashmiri goat that lives at elevations of 18,000 feet (5,500 m). The goat's fleece yields one of the world's finest wools, famous for its lavish softness and resilience. Herds of sheep and yaks also provide wool and meat.

Tradition records that men did most of the knitting. Floral sprigs or paisleys gaily patterned a background of white, black, or red on headgear, gloves, and socks.

Kashmiri Mittens

The floral motif in these mittens comes from knitted Kashmiri shawls found in the world's highest inhabited lands, the Himalayas.

Finished Size: 8" (20.5 cm) around by 7 $\frac{1}{2}$" (19.5 cm) long, excluding cuff.
Materials: 4 oz (113.5 g) cream sport-weight wool; $\frac{1}{2}$ oz (14 g) each blue and red sport-weight wool; $\frac{1}{4}$ oz (7 g) yellow sport-weight wool; size 2 (2.75 mm) double-pointed needles.
Gauge: 18 sts = 2" (5 cm).

Mitten body: With cream, CO 60 sts. Join. Work 2x1 rib for desired length, then change to body pattern and inc 12 sts evenly spaced—72 sts. On next rnd,

Kashmiri Mittens

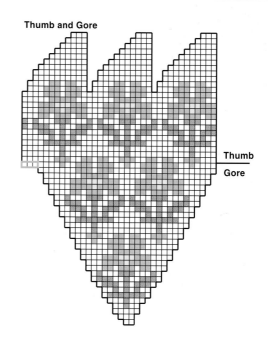

Thumb and Gore

Thumb

Gore

Kashmiri Mittens

Floral patterned mittens offer gay contrast to scattered rocks on the frozen peaks of "the roof of the world".

Kashmiri Mittens

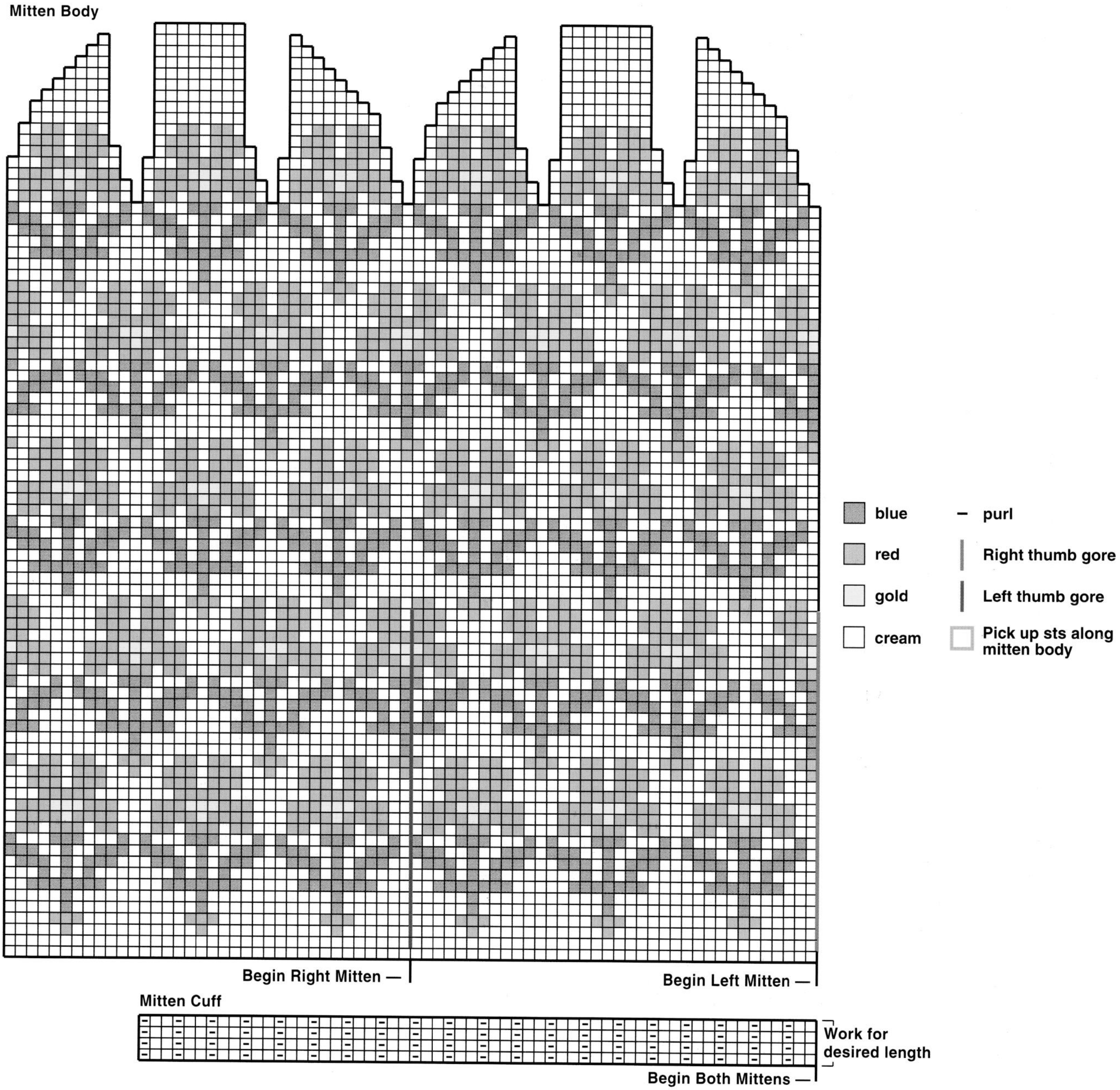

Mitten Body

▨ blue	— purl
▧ red	┃ Right thumb gore
☐ gold	┃ Left thumb gore
☐ cream	☐ Pick up sts along mitten body

Begin Right Mitten —   Begin Left Mitten —

Mitten Cuff

Work for desired length

Begin Both Mittens —

begin side seam thumb gore and work as charted for 30 rnds—33 thumb sts. Place thumb sts on yarn length. Rejoin and cont as charted or until piece measures to tip of little finger. Work decs as charted. Graft rem 16 sts with Kitchener st. *Thumb:* Place thumb sts on needles, pick up 3 sts, and join—36 sts. Work as charted or until piece measures to middle of thumbnail. Work 3-point dec as charted. Draw up rem sts.

Pakistan and Afghanistan

The neighboring countries of Afghanistan and Pakistan are arguably the home of the world's most ancient knitting traditions. Most of the region is mountainous, with tracts of arid desert. The oldest knitting in the world has been found preserved in the dry air and warm sands of these deserts.

The inhabitants of these two Asia Minor countries are primarily farmers and shepherds. In the vast, cold mountainous regions, elaborately patterned boot linings, gloves, and leggings featured patterns borrowed from ancient woven rugs.

In the desert, nomadic shepherds follow their flocks of goats and sheep on camelback in search of pastures and water. Knitted socks worn with sandals suit travel in hot sands. These socks are still knit today in patterns a thousand years old. Using the Eastern method of knitting in the direction of the heart, they are traditionally knit in tan and black with bright accents.

Mittens from Pakistan

This design is more than 1,000 years old and was typically used in men's footwear.

Finished Size: 8 ½" (21.5 cm) around by 7 ¼" (18.5 cm) long, excluding cuff.

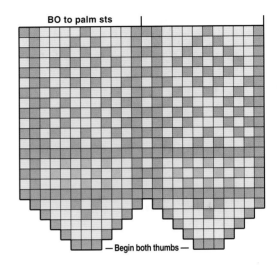

Mittens from Pakistan

Thumb

BO to palm sts

— Begin both thumbs —

Mittens from Pakistan

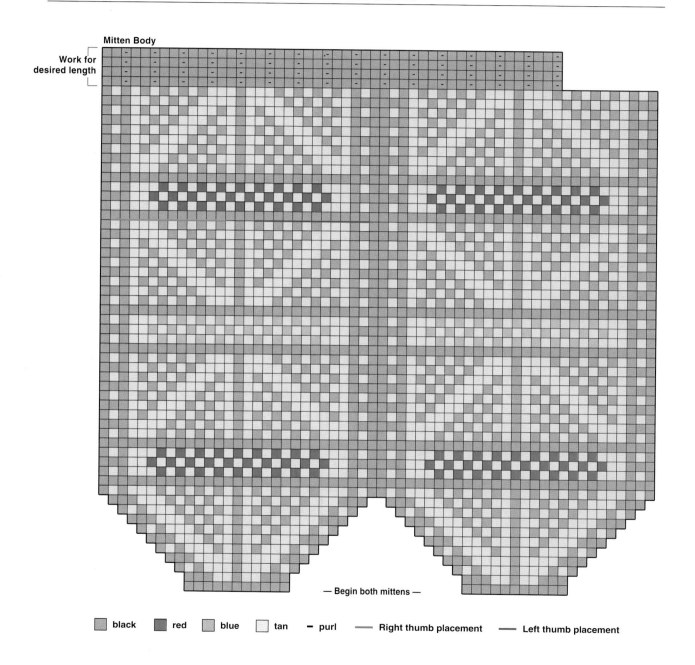

Mitten Body

Work for desired length

— Begin both mittens —

■ black ■ red ■ blue □ tan - purl — Right thumb placement — Left thumb placement

Materials: 2 oz (56.5 g) black worsted-weight wool; 1 oz (28.5 g) tan worsted-weight wool; $\frac{1}{2}$ oz (7 g) each red and blue worsted-weight wool; size 4 (3.5 mm) double-pointed needles.

Gauge: 14 sts = 2" (5 cm).

Thumb: With black and using the Eastern knitting method (see Techniques, page 16), CO 6 sts. Work flat incs as charted—24 sts. Cont as charted, then place sts on 2 holders (12 sts each). **Mitten body:** With black and using the Eastern Knitting method, CO 22 sts. Join. Work incs as charted until there are 58 sts. Cont to thumb insertion. Attach thumb by binding off 12 inner thumb sts with 12 palm sts. On next rnd, work rem 12 outer thumb sts over the 12 BO sts —58 sts. Work to end of body pattern, then dec 10 sts evenly spaced—48 sts. Work 2x1 rib for desired length. BO all sts loosely.

milkweed. Settlers of European or English descent introduced sheep to the Salish people in the mid-nineteenth century.

Salish garments are made of lofty handspun wool knit to a bulky gauge, giving them a heavy-weight warmth. The patterning is worked in five or, less often, three bands. Salish knitters use only natural colors, which they consider more pleasing to the eye. Traditionally, three colors are used. Two of the colors, often black and white, make up the design bands. The third color, used as background to separate the bands, is traditionally worked in a heathered yarn made by carding together the other two colors. Because making heathered wool is time-consuming, a third distinct color is more often used today. Done properly, there are no loose floats on the backside of Salish knitting; any yarn not in use is caught up with

Mittens from North America

Canada

The Salish tribe lives in Canada's beautiful Pacific southwest province of British Columbia, an area rich in forests and wildlife. When Europeans began to settle there, they encountered a people highly skilled in weaving. When introduced to knitting, the Cowichan band of the Salish tribe quickly embraced it, using geometric designs adapted from their weaving and basketry to develop a knitting tradition distinctly their own. They also designed motifs depicting important elements of their lives such as the thunderbird and revered whale. Their traditional yarns were spun from goat and dog hair supplemented with vegetative fibers ranging from Indian hemp and stinging nettles to the down of fireweed, cattail, and

Salish Mittens

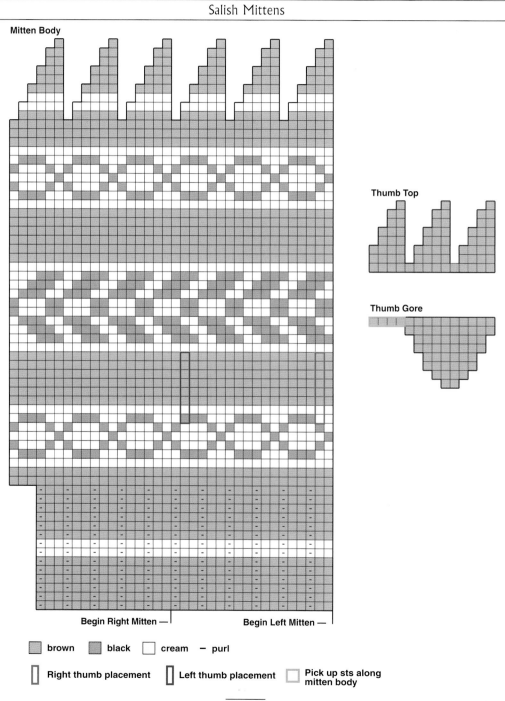

Mitten Body

Thumb Top

Thumb Gore

Begin Right Mitten —

Begin Left Mitten —

	brown		black		cream	- purl

| | Right thumb placement | | Left thumb placement | | Pick up sts along mitten body |

every stitch being made to increase the density of the fabric. A healthy cottage industry of Salish knitting is still active today.

Salish Mittens

The Salish use heavy-weight natural wool to create a hard-wearing mitten with ethnic charm.

Finished Size: 9" (23 cm) around by 7 ¾" (19.5 cm) long, excluding cuff.
Materials: 4 ½ oz (127.5 g) brown bulky-weight wool; 1 ½ oz (42.5 g) cream bulky weight wool; 1 oz (28.5 g) black bulky-weight wool; size 6 (4 mm) double-pointed needles.
Gauge: 8 sts = 2" (5 cm).

Mitten body: With brown, CO 33 sts. Join. Work 2x1 rib as charted or for desired length, then change to body pattern and inc 3 sts evenly spaced—36 sts. Work as charted for 6 more rnds. On next rnd, begin normal thumb gore and work as charted for 8 rnds—10 thumb sts. Place thumb sts on yarn length. Cont across rnd, CO 1 st over held thumb sts, and rejoin—36 sts. Work as charted or until piece measures to tip of little finger. Work 6-point dec as charted. Draw up rem sts. **Thumb:** Place thumb sts on needle, pick up 4 sts along the mitten body, and join—14 sts. Work even until piece measures to middle of thumbnail. Work 3-point dec as charted. Draw up rem sts.

Greenland and the United States

Greenland, the world's largest island, was named by Norse explorers for its green west coast and in hopes of attracting settlers. In reality, glaciers cover 85 percent of the land. During the four months of winter, there is no sunshine, the snowfall is heavy, and the polar winds are sharp. The native nomadic seal hunters who traveled and hunted here by dogsled, kayak, or on foot depended on warm, well-constructed garments for their survival.

The earliest traditional mittens in Greenland were constructed of animal skins. Knitting, introduced in the nineteenth century, made use of numerous fiber types, including hare, sheep, dog, fox, musk-ox, and even polar bear. Hare fiber was most popular because it was plentiful and yielded very smooth yarn that was pleasant to the skin. In addition, its brilliant white was particularly favored by hunters who wanted to blend into the icy landscape.

Sheep are raised in Greenland for wool and meat production, but they do not thrive in the harsh climate. Shepherds bring them indoors for their protection during the frequent bouts of extreme weather and sheep have sheltered in the barracks of abandoned American military bases.

Knitting in Greenland continues to flourish and evolve. The patterns of traditional beaded collars and wrist-warmers influence the designs, as do sweaters imported from northern Europe. Natural or salt-and-pepper yarns are used.

In the United States during the 1920s and 1930s, the proper young college woman was expected to be accomplished with her knitting needles. The stereotypical coed was healthy, efficient, and studious. She received good grades, swooned at the sight of a handsome young man, and was a whiz at sewing and knitting. Evenings, after studying, found her playing bridge with her knitting close at hand so that her turn at dummy could be put to productive use.

Students quickly identified professors who tolerated the click of needles in class. Balls of yarn were

encased in small flexible gadgets resembling minia-
ture bird cages that dangled off their wrists, allowing them to knit while in class or in transit between
buildings or back home to visit the folks. Most of
these women knit for themselves and their families.
A gift of knitting in a romance signified a higher level
of commitment to the relationship.

The stylish mittens of the day were made of white
or pastel angora wool. Yarn distributors advertised
that angora wool would knit up as "soft as a bunny—
yours for a little money." The angora fibers in mittens that had been placed in the refrigerator just before wearing would stick out and look fuzzy, as if the
wearer had handfuls of snow.

Mittens from Greenland and America

Mittens from Greenland and America

Greenland and the United States are an unlikely
early twentieth-century pair, yet these cozy white
mittens were knit in both countries. Greenland knitters used the fur of the abundant white hare, while
U.S. coeds chose angora.

Finished Size: 8" (20.5 cm) wide by 8" (20.5 cm)
  long, excluding cuff.
Materials: 2 oz (56.5 g) white mohair or angora; size
  2 (2.75 mm) double-pointed needles.
Gauge: 12 sts = 2" (5 cm).

Mitten body: CO 44 sts. Join. Work 2x2 rib for desired length, then change to body pattern and inc 4
sts evenly spaced—48 sts. Work as charted for 4 more

Thumb Top

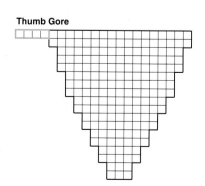

Thumb Gore

Mittens from Greenland and America

One Half Mitten Top

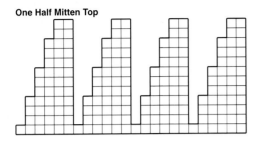

One Half Mitten Body

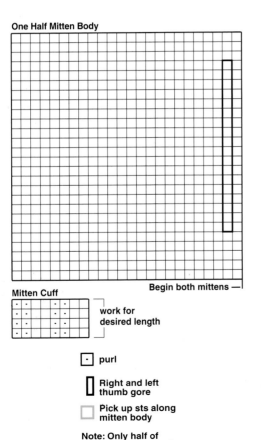

Begin both mittens —

Mitten Cuff

work for
desired length

☐• purl

▌ Right and left
thumb gore

☐ Pick up sts along
mitten body

Note: Only half of
the mitten body
and top sts are
charted.

rnds. On next rnd, begin normal thumb gore and work as charted for 18 rnds—17 thumb sts. Place thumb sts on yarn length. Cont across rnd, CO 1 st over held sts, and rejoin—48 sts. Work even until piece measures to tip of little finger. Work 8-point dec as charted. Draw up rem sts. **Thumb:** Place thumb sts on needles, pick up 4 sts along CO st along the mitten body, and join—21 sts. Work even until piece measures to middle of thumbnail. Work 3-point dec as charted. Draw up rem sts.

Minnesota

Mittens are a standard part of the wardrobe of children growing up in Minnesota, where winters are frigid and snow-filled. Sledding, skating, shoveling, and winter chores in the barn demand mittens that are both functional and warm. Generations of Minnesota mothers have knit a creative combination of a glove within a mitten with a mitten pocket to be drawn up and worn over the glove's fingers for added warmth. When separate fingers are needed, the mitten pocket is pulled back. Canadian women have also used this combination for many years, calling it a "Canadian glove".

Many of the earliest Europeans to settle in Minnesota were from Scandinavia and with them came their knitting traditions. One of their oldest was *tvåändsstickning*, in which two strands of the same yarn are alternated stitch for stitch. The technique gives the outward appearance of ordinary stockinette stitch and creates a very dense, warm fabric that is perfect for cold Minnesota winters. Tvåändsstickning may be used for part or all of the Minnesota mitten.

Tvåändsstickning is worked with two strands of the same yarn, traditionally the two ends of a single ball. One strand knits a stitch while the other travels behind. The other strand knits the next stitch while the first strand travels behind. Knitters created textured patterns by bringing one strand forward, purling it, allowing it to travel across the surface of the next stitch or stitches according to a charted pattern, purling it again, and then returning it to the back of the work. Some old Scandinavian patterns call for the two yarns to be twisted around each other before each stitch is worked, but this produces an inelastic fabric and is rarely used today. Allowing the strand to travel loosely behind the work yields a more flexible mitten with better insulating qualities and is easier.

Minnesota Mittens

Minnesota mittens combine the flexibility of gloves with the warmth of mittens for the best of both worlds. Tvåändsstickning adds warmth.

Finished Size: 8 ¼" (21 cm) around by 8 ¼" (21 cm) long, excluding cuff.
Materials: 4 ½ oz (127.5 g) worsted-weight wool; size 2 (2.75 mm) double-pointed needles.
Gauge: 12 sts = 2" (5 cm).

Mitten body: CO 48 sts. Join. Work 3x1 rib for desired length, then change to body pattern and inc 2 sts evenly spaced—50 sts. Begin tvåändsstickning and optional patterning and work 1 rnd. On next rnd, begin normal thumb gore and work as charted for 16 rnds—17 thumb sts. Place thumb sts on yarn length. Cont across rnd, CO 1 st over held thumb sts, and rejoin—50 sts. Knit 5 more rnds. Locate 25 front sts and 25 back sts and mark sides. Across back of mitten, pick up 1 st between each back st—24 new sts. Place new sts on yarn length. Rejoin and cont working original 50 sts until mitten body measures

to bottom of little finger. From one side, place 6 front sts and 5 back sts for later formation of little finger onto yarn length. CO 3 sts and rejoin—42 sts. Work for ¼" (6 mm). **Little finger:** Place little finger sts on needle, pick up 3 sts, and join—14 sts. Work even until piece measures to middle of fingernail. Work 5-point dec as charted. Draw up rem sts. **Ring finger:** Work on 6 front sts, 6 back sts, 3 sts picked up at base of little finger, and 3 sts CO over gap—18 sts. Work even until piece measures to middle of fingernail. Work 6-point dec as charted. Draw up rem sts. **Middle finger:** Work on 6 front sts, 6 back sts, 3 sts picked up at base of ring finger, and 3 sts CO sts over gap—18 sts. Work even until piece measures to middle of fingernail. Work 6-point dec as charted. Draw up rem sts. **Index finger:** Work on rem 15 sts and 3 sts picked up from base of middle finger—18 sts. Work even until piece measures to middle of fingernail. Work 6-point dec as charted. Draw up rem sts. **Thumb:** Place thumb sts on needle, pick up 3 sts, and join—20 sts. Work even until piece measures to

Minnesota Mittens

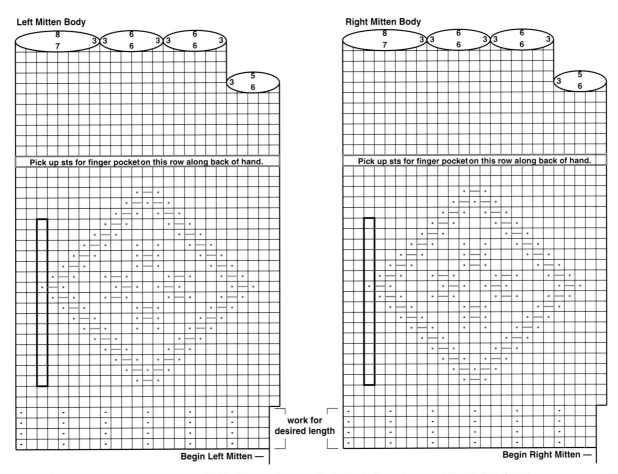

Left Mitten Body

Right Mitten Body

Pick up sts for finger pocket on this row along back of hand.

Begin Left Mitten —

Begin Right Mitten —

work for desired length

Right mitten: work across the back, placing pattern, work thumb, then the palm.
Left mitten: work across the palm, work thumb, then the back, placing pattern.

• purl with first thread

— purling thread travels in front of work (see instructions)

— purl

☐ Pick up sts along mitten body

Minnesota Mittens

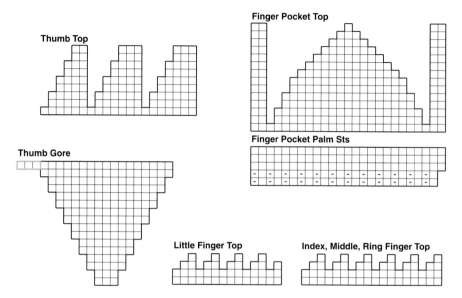

middle of thumbnail. Work 3-point dec as charted. Draw up rem sts. **Finger pocket:** Place 24 held sts on 2 needles. On a third needle, CO 24 sts and join—48 sts. Work 1x1 rib on palm side and St st on back side for 2 rnds, then inc 1 st each side—50 sts. Work even until same length as beg of decs on little finger. Work flat dec as charted. Draw up rem sts.

Reverse finger positions for other mitten.

Option: If you'd like to eliminate the fingertips, work the fingers until just past the first knuckle, or less, then dec 2 sts evenly spaced. Work 1x1 rib for 2 rnds. BO all sts loosely.

Colonial America

The colonial days of the European settlers in the United States can be summed up in the proverb "A man worked from sun to sun, but a woman's work was never done." Farm families' well-being depended upon the active participation of wives and daughters in the farm chores in addition to their home and kitchen duties. Garment manufacture was one of their many indispensable functions. Diaries from that time include endless chore lists and the number of inches that were knit before breakfast and by candlelight at night.

Knitting also went along with those working in the field. The township of Andover, Massachusetts, issued a decree in 1642 that those in the field watching cattle or sheep must spin or knit. Both knitting and spinning were considered productive substitutes for "larking". Though knitting was often a solitary pursuit, "bees" gathered neighbors to spin, knit, card, dye, and darn as well as exchange gossip and enjoy tea and treats.

Most children learned to knit at home at a young age. Prosperous New England families sent their children to dame schools run by poor widows to learn knitting and master the alphabet, hornbook, and Bible.

Mittens from Colonial New England

A verse from the Bible winds up the body of one mitten and finishes on the other.

Like socks, mittens were utilitarian and decorative. Patterns reflected the knitter's English or European roots. One apparently American original was to knit in the alphabet or a favorite poem or Bible verse which wound up the body of one mitten and finished on the other. Names and dates were also included. They were knit in wool or linsey-woolsey, a fiber made of flax or cotton and wool.

Mittens from Colonial New England

The verse on these mittens reads:

Do not store up for yourselves treasures here on earth, where moth and rust destroy and thieves break in and steal. But store up for yourselves treasures in heaven, where moth and rust do not destroy and thieves do not break in and steal, for where your treasure is there your heart will be also. . . But seek first His kingdom and His righteousness and all these things will be given to you.

St. Matthew 6:19–21, 33

Right Thumb and Gore

Thumb

Gore

Left Thumb and Gore

Thumb

Gore

Alphabet

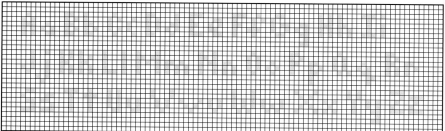

Mittens from Colonial New England

Left Mitten Body

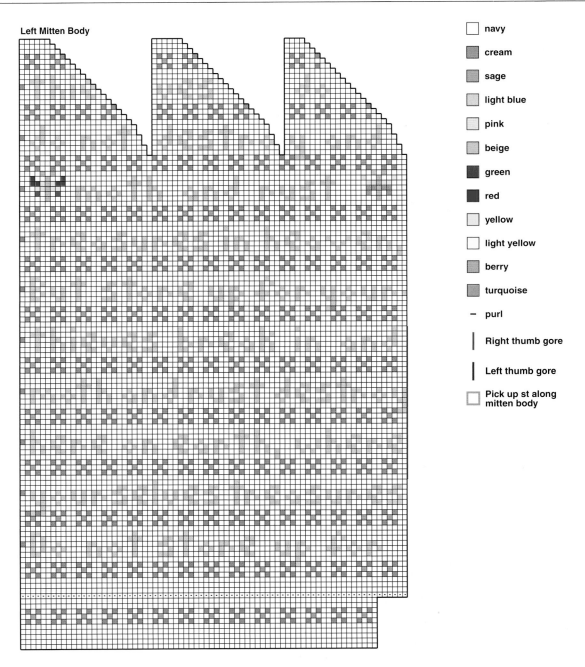

☐	navy
▦	cream
▦	sage
▦	light blue
▦	pink
▦	beige
■	green
■	red
☐	yellow
☐	light yellow
▦	berry
▦	turquoise
–	purl
│	**Right thumb gore**
│	**Left thumb gore**
☐	**Pick up st along mitten body**

Mittens from Colonial New England

Right Mitten Body

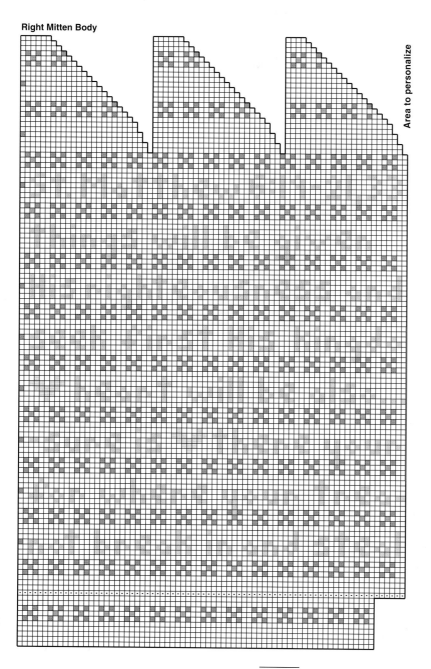

Area to personalize

Any verse or poem may be stitched into your mitten. Remember to line up the thumb and include it as your message winds up the hand. Use Swiss darning to add small motifs to lend interest to blank spaces and finish the tails of letters that hang down into the flower rows. Don't forget to add your name, date, and hometown for prosperity.

I began knitting these mittens while living among the rolling hills of southeast Ohio that were bursting with spring. The hills were covered with every shade of green and served as a beautiful backdrop for the creamy white four-petal blossoms of the dogwood tree. The trees were a heritage from the early European settlers, who enjoyed their beauty and hardiness. In their memory, I added flowers to my mittens. Later in the summer I was also charmed by the delicate four-petaled pink blossoms of the old-fashioned Sweet Briar rose, which could be substituted for the dogwood blossoms.

Finished Size: 8" (20.5 cm) around by 9 ¾" (25 cm) long.

Materials: 2 ½ oz (70 g) navy sport-weight wool; ½ oz (14 g) light sport-weight wool; ½ oz (14 g) total in flower colors sport-weight wool; size 1 (2.25 mm) double-pointed needles.

Gauge: 19 sts = 2" (5 cm).

Mitten body: With navy, CO 70 sts. Join. Work hem as charted, then purl 1 rnd, inc 6 sts evenly spaced—76 sts. Work as charted for 22 more rnds. On next rnd, begin side seam thumb gore and work as charted for 30 rnds—29 thumb sts. Place thumb sts on yarn length. Rejoin and cont as charted until piece measures to tip of little finger. Work 3-point dec as charted. Draw up rem sts. **Thumb:** Place thumb sts on needle, pick up 2 sts along mitten body, and join—31 sts. Work as charted or until piece mea-sures to middle of thumbnail. Work 3-point dec as charted. Draw up rem sts.

Mittens from South America
The Andean Mountains

The Andean mountains that run through Ecuador, Peru, and Bolivia have peaks that reach over 20,000 feet (6,100 m). They are home to shepherds, miners, and farmers who require warm, dependable clothing.

Ancient Inca fibers from the alpaca and llama produce beautiful and functional garments known for their bulky warmth. The alpaca and llama are closely related descendants from a common ancestor that lived during the Incan era. Alpacas were bred for soft fibers suitable for textile use, while llamas, with coarser wool, were used as pack animals. European settlers introduced sheep in the 1600s.

Knitting was introduced in the mid-1500s when Spanish explorers encountered the Incan civilization. The Incas were highly skilled weavers who quickly assimilated the portable craft of knitting. They carried it with them while shepherding animals and on long journeys hauling salt and other provisions through the mountains.

Andean knitting traditions are still alive today. The women and girls typically spin the wool. Both women and men participate in the family knitting, while women do the great bulk of knitting which is sold in the marketplace. Some areas choose bright hues while other regions prefer warm neutral colors. Stripes and various geometric shapes are commonly used.

Bulky-Weight Andean Mittens

The pattern of these mittens is similar to the bulky sweaters knit in the Andes. They include both natural and brightly dyed wools.

Bulky-Weight Andean Mittens

Mitten Body

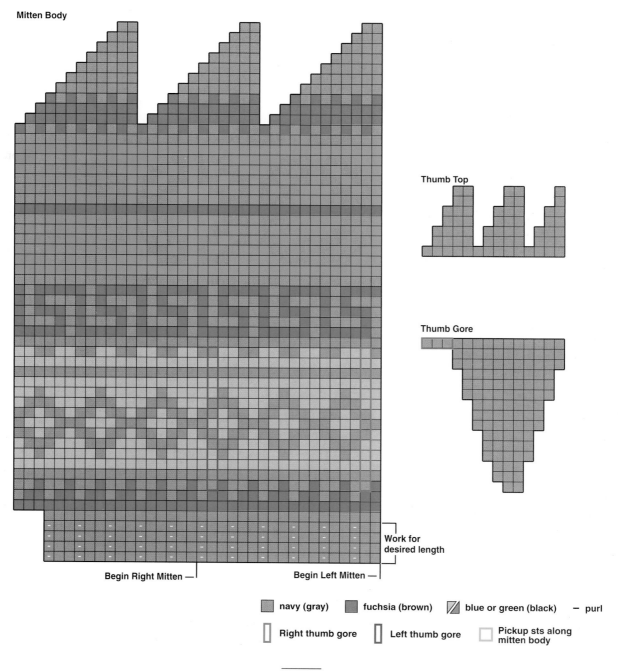

Thumb Top

Thumb Gore

Work for desired length

Begin Right Mitten —

Begin Left Mitten —

| navy (gray) | fuchsia (brown) | blue or green (black) | — purl |

| Right thumb gore | Left thumb gore | Pickup sts along mitten body |

Finished Size: 8" (20.5 cm) around by 8" (20.5 cm) long, excluding ribbing.

Materials: 3 oz (85 g) navy (gray) bulky-weight wool; 2 oz (56.5 g) blue and green (black) bulky-weight wool; 1 oz (28.5 g) fuchsia (brown) bulky-weight wool; size 5 (3.75 mm) double-pointed needles.

Gauge: 9 sts = 2" (5 cm).

Mitten body: With navy (gray), CO 33 sts. Join. Work 2x1 rib for desired length, then change to body pattern and inc 3 sts evenly spaced—36 sts. Cont as charted for 1 more rnd. On next rnd, work normal thumb gore as charted for 14 rnds—11 thumb sts. Place thumb sts on yarn length. Cont across rnd, CO 1 st over held thumb sts, and rejoin. Work as charted until piece measures to tip of little finger. Work 3-point dec as charted. Draw up rem sts.

Thumb: Place thumb sts on needle, pick up 3 sts along CO st along the mitten body, and join—14 sts. Work even until piece measures to middle of thumbnail. Work 3-point dec as charted. Draw up rem sts.

The Andean Altiplano

The *altiplano* regions are the high arid plateaus that stretch from southern Peru to central Bolivia and lie about 12,000 feet (3,658 m) above sea level. Here a unique knitting style uses a design system dating from pre-Columbian Incan times. The complex, tightly patterned motifs in a basketful of bright colors reveal how heavily the local weaving influences the knitting. Rows of orderly dark/light striped squares and rectangles are fitted with tiny motifs including cats, llamas, mythical beasts, flowers, and a myriad of bird forms.

Originally worked in natural fibers, today synthetic yarns are preferred because they are inexpensive, less labor-intensive, readily available, and most importantly, because the colors are much more intense than those that can be achieved with hand-dyed wool. The knitters re-spin the synthetic yarn by hand on drop spindles to add firmness and reduce pilling.

The most commonly knit item in boxed motifs is the *chullo* (chu-low), a cap with earflaps worn by men and children. Bicycle spokes are used to achieve a gauge varying between 18 and 42 stitches per 2" (5 cm). This produces a rigid fabric to block chilly highland winds. Much of knitting's usual stretch and elasticity is lost and caps can stand up by themselves in the shape of a cone. They are painstakingly stitched to fit. In some areas, the work is done from the inside, with all the stitches purled. This allows for more careful regulation of the tension of the many yarns being carried.

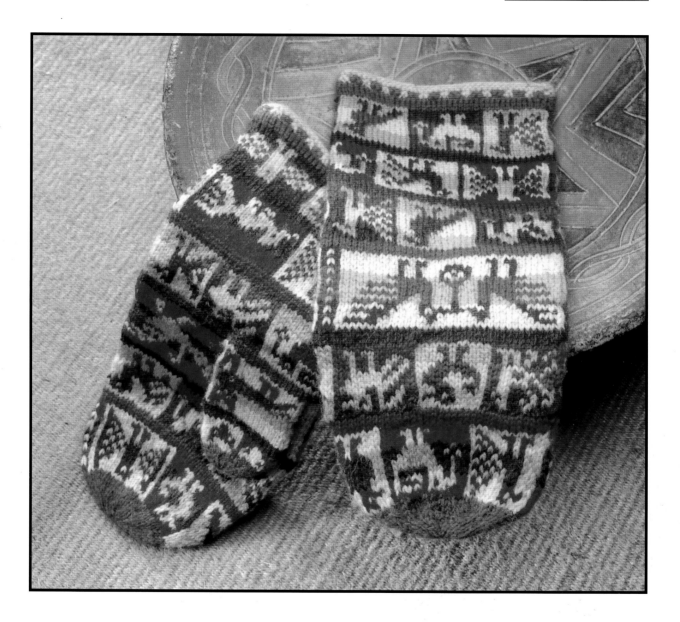

Andean Altiplano Mittens

*These mittens, knit at a gauge of 19 sts to 2" (5 cm), are of a rigid fabric
that will block chilly highland winds.*

Andean Altiplano Mittens

Mitten Body

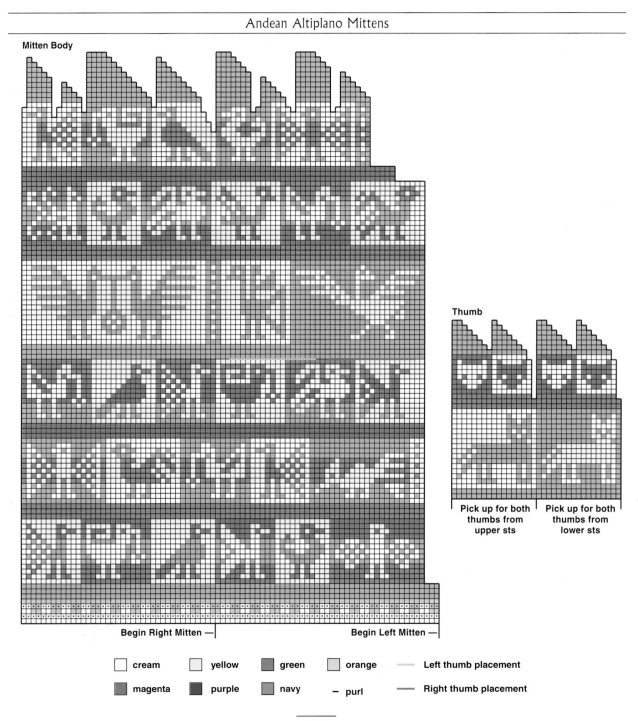

Thumb

Pick up for both thumbs from upper sts | Pick up for both thumbs from lower sts

Begin Right Mitten —| Begin Left Mitten —|

	cream		yellow		green		orange	—	Left thumb placement
	magenta		purple		navy	–	purl	—	Right thumb placement

Men and boys as young as eight design and knit their own caps, choosing colors such as deep purple, hot orange, pink, and royal blue. Colors may identify the wearer's region and community.

Andean Altiplano Mittens

These motifs come from Andean caps knit and worn by men and boys.

Finished Size: 8 ½" (21.5 cm) around by 9 ½" (24 cm) long.

Materials: 6 ½ oz (184 g) sport-weight yarn in bright colors; contrasting waste yarn; size 1 (2.25 mm) double-pointed needles.

Gauge: 19 sts = 2" (5 cm).

Mitten body: CO 84 sts. Join. Following chart, work 4 rnds in garter st, then 4 rnds in St st, dec 3 sts evenly spaced on last rnd—81 sts. Work as charted 45 more rnds. On next rnd, with contrasting waste yarn, mark placement of peasant thumb over 17 sts as shown. Rejoin and cont to top of mitten, working dec as charted. Draw up rem sts. *Thumb:* Remove waste yarn, place thumb sts on needles, and join—34 sts. Work as charted or until piece measures to middle of thumbnail. Work 4-point dec as charted. Draw up rem sts.

Other Mittens

Tweedledee and Tweedledum Mittens

Whimsical puppet mittens delighted many children during the 1960s. On long bus rides to school or huddled in snow igloos, children enjoyed mittens with personality as well as warmth.

The inspiration for these mittens, Tweedledee and Tweedledum, first came to life in 1872, when Lewis Carroll wrote the classic *Through the Looking Glass.*

Finished Size: 7" (18 cm) around by 5 ¾" (14.5 cm) long, excluding cuff.

Materials: 1 oz (28.5 g) each yellow and dark blue worsted-weight wool; ½ oz (14 g) white worsted-weight wool; small amounts of green, pink, brown, and red for small motifs; size 3 (3.25 mm) double-pointed needles.

Gauge: 12 sts = 2" (5 cm).

Mitten body: With yellow, CO 40 sts. Join. Work 2x2 rib for desired length, then change to body pattern and inc 2 sts evenly spaced—42 sts. Cont as charted for 2 more rnds. On next rnd, beg normal thumb gore and work as charted for 13 rnds—13 thumb sts. Place thumb sts on yarn length. Cont

Tweedledee and Tweedledum Mittens

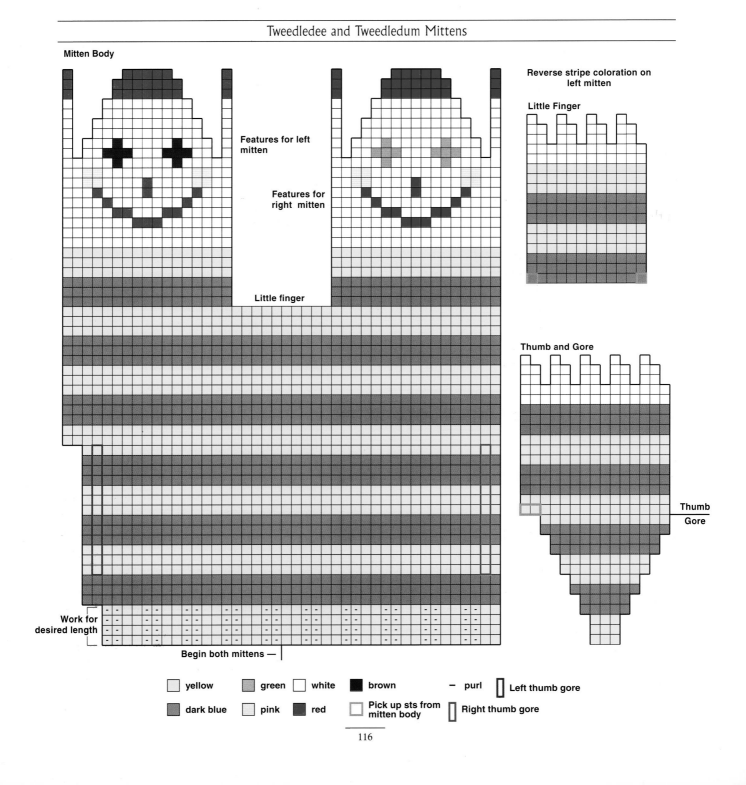

Mitten Body

Features for left mitten

Features for right mitten

Little finger

Reverse stripe coloration on left mitten

Little Finger

Thumb and Gore

Thumb

Gore

Work for desired length

Begin both mittens —

	yellow		green		white		brown	−	purl		Left thumb gore
	dark blue		pink		red		Pick up sts from mitten body				Right thumb gore

across rnd, CO 3 sts over held thumb sts, and re-join—44 sts. Work even until piece measures to base of little finger. Mark mitten sides. On one side place 5 front sts and 5 back sts, (10 sts total) on yarn length for later formation of little finger. CO 2 sts over gap, rejoin, and continue as charted until mitten body measures to tip of little finger. Work flat dec as chart-ed. Graft rem 14 sts with Kitchener st. **Thumb:** Place thumb sts on needles, pick up 2 sts, and rejoin—15 sts. Work as charted until piece measures to middle of thumbnail. Work 5-point dec as charted. Draw up rem sts. **Little finger:** Place little finger sts on nee-dles, pick up 2 sts, and rejoin—12 sts. Work as chart-ed until piece measures to middle of fingernail. Work 4-point dec as charted. Draw up rem sts.

Add face on palm side of mitten with Swiss darn-ing (see Techniques, page 19). Add hair by attach-ing loops of red yarn to top of mitten with a needle. The loops should be free-form and can be as long or as short as the mitten's personalities call for.

Miniature Mittens

For knitters with a passion for mittens, these minia-tures are especially fun to make. They can decorate the home, serve as Christmas tree ornaments, or warm the hands of a favorite doll. They measure about 2 ½" by 1 ½" (6.5 by 4 cm) when knit with worsted-weight wool and size 0 (2 mm) double-pointed nee-dles. Alter the size of the mittens by substituting larg-er or smaller needles and heavier or lighter wool.

These tiny mittens are knit in the Swedish pole, the Norwegian rose, and Iceland's Jacob's ladder patterns.

Finished Size: 3" (7.5 cm) around by 2 ½" (6.5 cm) long, including ribbing.

Materials: ½ oz (14 g) wool in two colors; size 1 (2.25 mm) double-pointed needles.

Gauge: 8 sts = 1" (2.5 cm) (Norwegian rose and Jacob's ladder, 1st notation); 9 sts = 1" (2.5 cm) (Pole, 2nd notation).

Mitten body: CO 22 sts. Join. Work 1x1 rib for desired length, then change to body pattern and inc 2 (4) sts evenly spaced—24 (26) sts. Work as chart-ed for 3 more rnds. On next rnd, place 4 (5) thumb sts on yarn length. Cont across rnd, and CO 4 (5) sts over held sts, and rejoin—24 (26) sts. Cont to top of chart, working decs as charted. Draw up rem sts. **Thumb:** Place thumb sts on needles, pick up 2 (1) st(s) in each corner, and join—12 sts. Work as chart-ed, beg decs when thumb measures ¾" (2 cm). Draw up rem sts. Attach finger-knit mitten cord (see Tech-niques, page 18).

Miniature Mittens

Jacob's Ladder Thumb

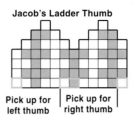

Pick up for
left thumb   Pick up for
right thumb

Jacob's Ladder Mitten Body

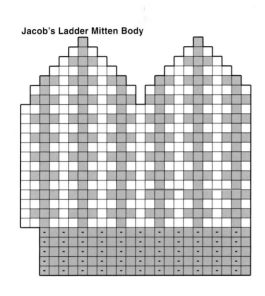

Norwegian Rose Thumb

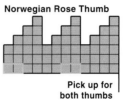

Pick up for
both thumbs

Swedish Pole Thumb

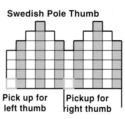

Pick up for
left thumb   Pickup for
right thumb

— Right thumb placement

— Left thumb placement

- purl

Swedish Pole Mitten Body

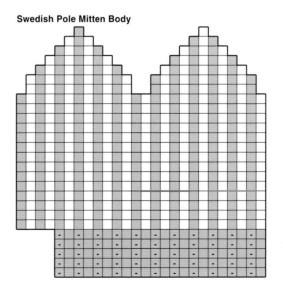

Norwegian Rose Mitten Body

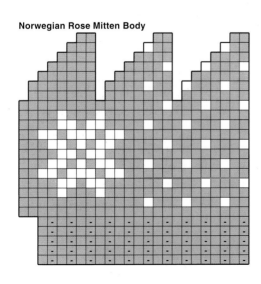